T0010323

SEEING
THE
UNSEEN

SEEING
— THE —
UNSEEN
BEYOND PREJUDICES,
PARADIGMS, AND PARTY LINES

MARK M. BECKWITH

FOREWORD BY SHANE CLAIBORNE

Morehouse Publishing
NEW YORK

Copyright © 2022 by Mark M. Beckwith

All rights reserved. No part of this book may be reproduced, stored in a retrieval system, or transmitted in any form or by any means, electronic or mechanical, including photocopying, recording, or otherwise, without the written permission of the publisher.

Unless otherwise noted, the Scripture quotations contained herein are from the New Revised Standard Version Bible, copyright © 1989 by the Division of Christian Education of the National Council of Churches of Christ in the U.S.A. Used by permission. All rights reserved.

Morehouse Publishing, 19 East 34th Street, New York, NY 10016

Morehouse Publishing is an imprint of Church Publishing Incorporated.

Page 88: Mandorla, or Vesica Piscis—Stock photo ID: 1222755329. Credit: vavit. Reprinted by permission.

Page 103: The Anastasis fresco—Stock photo ID: 845636536. Credit Zzvet. Reprinted by permission.

Pages 183–184: Julia Esquivel, "They Have Threatened Us with Resurrection," translated by Ann Woehrle, © 1982, 1994. By permission of Brethren Press.

Cover design by Jennifer Kopec, 2Pug Design

Typeset by Newgen

Library of Congress Cataloging-in-Publication Data

Names: Beckwith, Mark M., author.
Title: Seeing the unseen : beyond prejudices, paradigms, and party lines / Mark M. Beckwith.
Description: New York, NY : Morehouse Publishing, [2022] | Includes bibliographical references.
Identifiers: LCCN 2021048828 (print) | LCCN 2021048829 (ebook) | ISBN 9781640655188 (paperback) | ISBN 9781640655195 (epub)
Subjects: LCSH: Conflict management—Religious aspects—Christianity. | Communication—Religious aspects—Christianity. | Thought and thinking—Religious aspects—Christianity. | Listening—Religious aspects—Christianity.
Classification: LCC BV4597.53.C58 B43 2022 (print) | LCC BV4597.53.C58 (ebook) | DDC 248—dc23/eng/20211130
LC record available at https://lccn.loc.gov/2021048828
LC ebook record available at https://lccn.loc.gov/2021048829

To Henri Nouwen (1932–1996)—teacher and mentor,
and to the Rev. Canon Ed Rodman—mentor and colleague.

Each of whom, at different times and in different ways,
helped me see the unseen.

CONTENTS

FOREWORD

There is something more important than having new ideas, and that is having new eyes.

That's why I am so excited about this book by my friend Mark Beckwith. This book is all about having new eyes.

Years ago I had the opportunity to work with Mother Teresa in India, where I spent some time in a village of folks who had leprosy. In the caste system, they were literally "outcasts"—not allowed in stores or restaurants . . . pushed to the margins of society, untouchable, invisible. But Mother Teresa knew better. She knew they were children of God, made in the image of God . . . and if Jesus is right that the last will be first, these folks certainly had a special place in the family of God. So she started this little village outside Calcutta where about 150 families lived. They grew their own food, made their own clothes, ran their own school. While I was there, my job was to take piles of their homegrown cotton and roll cotton balls for the clinic, which was by the railroad tracks. The doctors in the clinic were all survivors of leprosy and were now providing treatment for others still infected by the disease. One day, after I had been there a while, one of the doctors had to leave early, and he asked me to take his place.

I came forward, sat in the doctor's seat, and began staring intently, deeply into the next patient's eyes. I didn't speak Hindi, and he didn't know much English, but we connected, and I tried to ensure his trust with a gentle smile. I began carefully dressing the man's wound. He stared at me with such intensity that it felt like he was looking into my soul. Every once in a while, he would slowly close his eyes.

When I was finished wrapping his wound, he smiled as he looked into my eyes and said this word: "Namaste." One of the men in the clinic that day explained to me the profound meaning of the word. He said that we don't have a good English translation that captures the full power of the word, but it essentially means "I see you. I love you. I recognize the image of God in you." In his words: "The Spirit of God in me loves the Spirit of God that I see in you."

I will never forget getting lost in that man's eyes as we sat in the clinic there on the railroad tracks. I knew that I had not just looked into the eyes of some pitiful leper in Calcutta but that I had gazed into the eyes of Jesus, and he had not seen just some rich, do-gooder white kid from America but the image of God in me. I had seen Jesus in him, and he in me. I saw a clearer glimpse of Jesus in this leper's eyes than I have ever seen in any stained-glass window or religious icon.

Looking into the eyes of another person may be the clearest glimpse of God many of us get in this world.

At the heart of this wonderful book is an invitation to see people differently and to see the world differently. Mark draws on his own experiences and some of the giants of compassion over the centuries. He does a deep dive into scripture and takes his cues from Jesus.

This book reminds me of the works of Martin Buber. In *I and Thou*, the brilliant European thinker speaks of how we can see a person as simply a material object, something you look at, an "it"—or we can look into a person and enter the sacredness of their humanity so that they become a "Thou." (And as a Jewish philosopher who immigrated to Palestine to advocate for Arab-Jewish cooperation, Buber knew all too well how easily we objectify and demonize others.)

All the time, we look *at* people—celebrities, rock stars, migrant workers, homeless folks. We see Black, white, Asian. We see male, female, gay, straight. But over time, we can develop new eyes and look *into* people. We can enter the Holiest of Holies through their eyes. They can become a "Thou." This book is a training manual for how to see the world differently, and how to see people differently.

In the murderers, we see our own capacity to harm. In the addicts, we see our own addictions. In the saints, we catch glimpses of our own holiness. We can see our own brokenness, our own violence, our own ability to destroy, and we can see our own sacredness, our own capacity to love and forgive. When we realize that we are both wretched and beautiful, we are freed up to see others the same way.

We are all made of the same dust. We cry the same tears.

I saw this happen when the man whispered that sacred Hindi word *namaste*. And I saw it in Iraq, when people put their hands over their hearts as a sign of respect and recognition. In South Africa, I also learned about *ubuntu*, which is a similar idea. It means, "I cannot be all that I am meant to be until you are everything you are meant to be." We do not live in isolation. An injury to one is an injury to all. And until all of us are free, none of us are free.

We are living in turbulent times, in an age of deep division and paralyzing polarization. Lots of people are talking at each other but not with each other. It is clear that white Americans and people of color are experiencing a different America. It can feel impossible to imagine a healthy future together when we aren't even sharing the same narrative about our past. We hear it in the culture wars around critical race theory and we witness it in the tearing down of Confederate statues.

Around the world we encounter crisis after crisis with tragedies and death tolls, and it is easy to get lost and overwhelmed by it all. So where do we start?

In this beautiful book, Mark invites us to start by *seeing*—not just looking *at* people but looking deeply *into* them. He invites us to listen deeply to those who are hurting, even to those with whom we disagree.

I am reminded of how many times Jesus said the words "to those who have the eyes to see and the ears to hear." Mark helps us learn how to see better and listen better. In this book, he helps us develop a special kind of "night vision" that is going to be essential in the dark days ahead. We are going to need to be able to see in the dark.

And we are going to need to be able to see not just with our eyes but also with our hearts, our souls. This book is going to help us navigate this complicated world in the days ahead.

This is not just a book you read with your eyes . . . it is a book you read with your heart.

Shane Claiborne

Coauthor of *Common Prayer: A Liturgy for Ordinary Radicals*

SEEING
THE
UNSEEN

INTRODUCTION

We are trained to think. Going back centuries, our Western educational system has been devoted to enabling people to achieve a level of mastery by expanding their ability to think. The three Rs—reading, (w)riting, and (a)rithmetic—have served as the building blocks for young people to expand their thinking, with the goal of being better able to participate in commerce and community.

And it has worked. Advances in science and technology, mathematics, and medicine have demonstrated that the emphasis on thinking has paid off. We know more. We think better and more clearly.

Yet this trajectory of better thinking has led many to believe that if we are not masters of the universe, then we are at least rapidly approaching the point where we can be effective shepherds of it. Despite the COVID-19 pandemic, climate crisis, governments in chaos and collapse, and increasing polarization, we still harbor the hubris that we can manage it all.

Our cultural emphasis on thinking has not been applied to our ability to see. To be sure, our advanced thinking has enabled us to treat our eyes more expertly—from sophisticated eyeglass lenses to effective treatments for cataracts, glaucoma, and macular degeneration to rapid expansion of laser surgery. But we are not trained and truly enabled to see the world's fullness— its pain and joy, compassion and cruelty. We regularly get glimpses of pain and joy, but they are often limited in such a way so as to reinforce our thinking.

And how we think is part of the problem with how we see. The European Renaissance (roughly between 1300 and 1700) generated remarkable advances in art, science, and mathematics. Thinking became more focused and valued. Philosophical and theological support for this expanded ability to understand the workings of the world was largely provided by René Descartes (1596–1650), widely regarded as the founder of modern Western philosophy. While this book is not a discourse on Western philosophy, Descartes's work has deeply affected how we have been trained to see (or not to see). Descartes summarized his philosophy as *cogito, ergo sum* (I think, therefore I am). This dictum sets up a separation between self and other, not to mention an emphasis on individualism. A subject's ability to think provides the opportunity to master. On one level, Descartes's philosophy has served us well. On another level, it has caused some significant problems.

Psychohistorians have provided a plausible and compelling context for Descartes's mindset. René was fourteen when the king of France, Henry IV, was assassinated in 1610. Known as Henry the Great, the king made a commitment to ensuring that all his subjects had enough food to eat. He was also a champion of religious tolerance, allowing for the establishment of both Catholic and Protestant churches in the country, and supporting both religious expressions. Raised a Protestant, Henry converted to Catholicism and back again several times in his lifetime. His religious openness created enemies, one of whom, a religious fanatic, attacked the king's carriage on the back streets of Paris and stabbed Henry to death.

For many in France, including a young René, hope died with the king. As was the custom of the day, the heart of the king was removed and put on display for three days at Saint Louis Church in Paris so people could come and pay homage. A teenage René joined the line of mourners. According to this thread of psychohistory, when he saw the king's heart, it broke his own, and he made a vow that he would never allow his heart to be that vulnerable again. Ergo, Descartes's despair led to a philosophical construct that created as much distance from the emotional workings of the heart as possible: Thinking would reign. And seeing—at least seeing accompanied by an emotional valence—was either minimized or its emotional import was abandoned altogether. Hence our own problems in seeing the world in its fullness today—and the problems that this lack of seeing creates.

One of the reasons I strongly relate to this interpretation of history is that it helps explain my own inability—and in some cases, my unwillingness—to see the fullness of the world. For fourteen years I served a church in Worcester, Massachusetts. I drove to the church most every day, and it was often the case that my short commute was interrupted by a school bus stopping to pick up a load of students. I saw the bus, occasionally cursed at it for causing me to wait—and was effectively blind to the children waiting to get on board.

Several years into my tenure at the church, for reasons that I cannot explain, there was a day when I was finally able to shift my view from the bus to the kids who were waiting for it. And there were a lot of them— I was surprised to see the number of them because I couldn't imagine that there were that many kids living in that neighborhood, which was economically challenged. I could readily see the physical degradation of the neighborhood that surrounded the urban church I served, but I didn't want to *think* that vulnerable children lived there. There wasn't enough space for them to live, I thought, and what space there was seemed woefully inadequate. My mind didn't want me to see the young people in that place, so I didn't. Until, of course, I did—and my commute became more difficult because I could now see, in greater relief, the economic injustice that enveloped the neighborhood where I spent so much of my time.

I would like to think that my heart has never been cauterized. It has always reached out to others. I have readily empathized with other people's pain. For as long as I can remember, I have wanted to help ease that pain. A noble trait, I believe, one that many others share, but that day I learned that my empathy had been limited by what I had been trained to see, and what my thinking allowed me to see.

After my junior year in college, our glee club went on a singing tour of several countries in Africa. One of our stops was in southern Zambia. We sang near the source of Victoria Falls, one of the most spectacular places I have ever seen. The day after the concert, our bus dropped us off at one end of a very high bridge that spanned the Zambezi River, which forms the boundary between Zambia and what was then Rhodesia (now Zimbabwe). We walked out to the middle of the bridge to get a better view of the river far below. Coming to us from the Rhodesia side was a small but steady stream of people, which included a young, presumably Rhodesian, mother with her two young children. They were carrying several large suitcases. My heart went out to them, and I walked over and offered to help. Without receiving a reply, I picked up the largest suitcases and accompanied them to the Zambian side. I then gave the luggage back to the mother, and while there wasn't a verbal acknowledgment of my assistance, I could tell she was relieved. I took it as gratitude.

It wasn't until a long time later that I realized that she was more likely hiding her fear—she probably initially regarded my help as an aggressive act by a white man who was taking her luggage, her children, and herself to a place of danger. When I returned her luggage, no doubt she was relieved—not for my help, but because I had not committed yet another one of the racist acts that were standard practice in the country she was coming from. I hadn't seen that.

I have spent much of my life since then trying to open my eyes and my heart to injustice and blessing—to be able to see the broader context of a young family crossing a bridge from Rhodesia to Zambia—but my ambition, arrogance, and Cartesian-trained manner of thinking have often gotten in the way. The combination of finely honed thinking and cultural (not to mention male) arrogance has taught me to see things in a certain way. Several years ago, some colleagues and I watched a compelling video featuring Joel Barker, a futurist and business consultant. The video was drawn from Barker's book *Discovering the Future: The Business of Paradigms*, and it featured several examples of how established paradigms influence, if not control, how we see. At one point the video presented a series of playing cards in quick succession. Everything looked normal. The video then slowed down the presentation of the same cards, and Barker pointed out that all the spade and club cards were red and the heart and diamond cards were black. Rarely, he said, did a viewer pick up the switch, primarily because the paradigm of spades and clubs being black and hearts and diamonds being red is so ingrained in us that we can't see otherwise.

It is often the case, in our Cartesian-influenced Western world, that how we think shapes how we see, and how we see reinforces how we think. Thinking comes first—except when it doesn't. There are moments when our vision transcends boundaries and paradigms, and we are then able to see with our hearts—and our minds can follow by offering some context. During my first year of seminary, I read Thomas Merton's autobiographical trilogy: *The Seven Storey Mountain*, *Conjectures of a Guilty Bystander*, and *The Sign of Jonas*. I am among many who consider Thomas Merton to be the most influential Christian spiritual writer of the twentieth century. In *Conjectures of a Guilty Bystander*, Merton describes an unexpected vision he received during a visit to a doctor in Kentucky:

> In Louisville, at the corner of Fourth and Walnut, in the center of the shopping district, I was suddenly overwhelmed with the realization that I loved all these people, that they were mine and I theirs, that we could not be alien to one another even though we were total strangers. It was like waking from a dream of separateness, of spurious self-isolation in a special world. . . .
>
> This sense of liberation from an illusory difference was such a relief and such a joy to me that I almost laughed out loud. . . . I have the immense joy of being [hu]man, a member of a race in which God Himself became incarnate. As if the sorrows and stupidities of the human condition could overwhelm me, now that I realize what we all are. And if only everybody could realize this! But it cannot be explained. There is no way of telling people that they are all walking around shining like the sun.
>
> Then it was as if I suddenly saw the secret beauty of their hearts, the depths of their hearts where neither sin nor de-

sire nor self-knowledge can reach, the core of their reality, the person that each one is in God's eyes. If only they could all see themselves as they really are. If only we could see each other that way all the time. There would be no more war, no more hatred, no more cruelty, no more greed. . . . But this cannot be seen, only believed and "understood" by a peculiar gift. (*Conjectures of a Guilty Bystander*)

"If only we could see." Thank God that Merton did see in this moment of epiphany and was able to write it down, as this record has had a profound influence on millions of pilgrims, and even prompted the city of Louisville to put up a commemorative plaque at that site. I made a pilgrimage to that same intersection decades after Merton had his experience—and I waited for something to happen, for my eyes and heart to be opened in a similar way.

Nothing.

But Merton's ability to see—along with so many others like him (though perhaps not as articulate)—has given me a level of confidence and faith that seeing beyond thinking is possible, that a different vantage point can open us up to seeing injustice more clearly and experiencing blessing in new and unexpected ways.

Many years after my school bus epiphany, I became a bishop, and for several years I joined a growing cohort of Episcopalians from across the country who offered "Ashes to Go" on Ash Wednesday. My colleague and I would position ourselves at strategic points at Penn Station in Newark, New Jersey. Another colleague would hold up a large sign that announced our presence and explained what we were offering—to apply ashes on the commuters' foreheads. People came forward, many more than we expected. As I reflected on the interactions, I came away with the realization that people wanted not only to observe this ancient ritual, but also to be blessed.

And so I went back to Newark's Penn Station at other times of the year to offer blessings, which a surprising number of people were willing to receive. I made it a point of showing up to offer "Blessings to Go" every September 11, which felt like a day of profound vulnerability, given that the World Trade Center had been easy to see from many points in Newark (some ten miles away) and many people commuted to lower Manhattan. I expected that the presence of police officers with AR-15s draped over their shoulders and the well-trained but fierce-looking police dogs accompanying them heightened that vulnerability.

Yet, during one of these visits, I noticed that most people didn't seem to be paying much attention to the beefed-up security. They were too busy trying to catch a train or a bus—or zeroing in on their cellphones. In the midst of the chaos and cacophony, the first verses of Revelation 21 seeped into my heart and brain: "Then I saw a new heaven and a new earth. . . . And I saw the holy city, the new Jerusalem, coming down out of heaven from God, prepared as a bride adorned for her husband" (Revelation 21:1–2). And then the passage filtered up to my eyes, because that is what I saw—the new Jerusalem coming down out of heaven, in the bowels of Newark's Penn Station. In that strange moment, the commuting crowd became walking images of God's blessing, and we were all somehow uniquely related to one another. And as soon as I saw this vision, my brain kicked in with immediate pushback: New Jerusalem? In Newark? On 9/11? In all this confusion? I don't think so. You can't see that. Expunge the vision and the idea that spawned it.

But I held on to that vision. It was a vision of blessing as I set about the task of blessing others. And I found myself occasionally talking about my experience, sheepishly at first, because I thought people would think me too bizarre, or worse. But the more I talked about it, the more confidence I had that there was a holy presence there, in what the world would otherwise regard as an unholy place on an unholy day. Like Thomas Merton in Louisville, I felt a deep kinship with the crush of humanity that was going about its business on that September 11 morning. And I felt that we were all blessed.

* * *

This book is an invitation to see what we don't see. To see beyond our prejudices, paradigms, and hidebound thinking, all of which can shroud us from, if not blind us to, injustice. And to see moments when those veils of prejudice, paradigms, and thinking are mysteriously and wonderfully taken away and we can feel the blessing. Which then prompts us to share the blessing with others.

I continue to struggle to keep my eyes fully opened to see injustice and blessing. I take some comfort in the fact that our spiritual ancestors had similar difficulties, and I will talk about that (Luke 24). I have discovered that where we locate God—up in heaven, down here on earth, or no place at all (because for some it is a supreme challenge to imagine that God even exists in the first place)—has considerable bearing on how we see (or do not see) one another. I will talk about the categories we put people in, the confining arenas we put God in—and the language we use to reinforce our blindness and prejudice. I will draw on the wisdom of scripture, the challenges our spiritual ancestors faced, and the brilliance that Jesus and the prophets offered.

I will introduce the *mandorla*, the Italian word for almond, which is the visual representation of the intersection of two competing circles of ideas, positions, or movements. (Think of a Venn diagram from sixth-grade math.) Engaging the mandorla can free us from the paralysis of polarity and the myopia it generates. I will give examples of individuals and movements that have invited people into the mandorla space— where reconciliation and redemption can take place. There are traditions and practices that we have long engaged in that, if reconfigured, or shifted even a little bit, can deepen our commitment to justice and open us up to blessing.

One of the gifts I received in seminary was to have Henri Nouwen as a teacher, mentor, and friend. More than anyone else in my life, Henri—whose wisdom, insights, and heart were clearly manifested in his lectures and many books (thirty-nine in all, plus countless articles)— helped open my eyes and heart to a deeper appreciation of God's blessing and the compelling need for justice. Henri began nearly every lecture by suggesting that his audience not pay so much attention to what he said (or wrote) but to how his words stirred ideas and insights in the hearts and souls of those who were listening. Pay attention to that, Henri said.

Similarly, these insights and stories are offered to rouse insights and stories within you that are unique to you, and to help you see the unseen and experience anew the urgency for justice and an openness to blessing.

— PART I —

What We Don't See

1

LEARNING TO SEE

Where is God? Who is God? Is there a God? These are questions I have wrestled with for as long as I can remember. Over the course of my life, I have considered several answers. Some of those answers have been overly simple; others have been remarkably obtuse. Many have been somewhere in between. There have been times when I have been drawn to certain answers—and in hindsight, I can identify reasons for their appeal. But what has been consistent over the years is a growing appreciation of God's presence—in the world, and in my life. The challenge has been, and continues to be, discerning how and where God is present.

God spoke: "Don't make me come down there!"—or so said the billboard at the entrance to the Lincoln Tunnel, which connects New Jersey to New York City. This quotation can be found on church signs, billboards, and media posts all across the country. The implication is clear: God is an upset father who has had it with the disobedience and debauchery of his children. And God is threatening to come down from his heavenly perch and straighten us out. Punishment will no doubt be administered, and the intensity and pain of that punishment will depend on the egregiousness of our sins. So we had better listen—and obey.

When I was a young boy, God was not distant, but very close to me, even standing on my shoulder and watching every move I made. As a child, I cowered before God, whom I saw as big, stern, and quick to anger—a divine presence out to get me. Without having heard of Jonathan Edwards, whose "sinners in the hands of an angry God" sermon, which was first preached nearly two hundred fifty years ago and has in large measure framed American Protestant Christianity, I knew his warning, and I made every effort to comply. Because I thought that God could not only hear me, but also had access to what I thought, I felt the need to curate my thoughts, and I tried to keep myself as pure and obedient as possible so as to avoid God's considerable wrath.

One of my first God-related memories is of tears about having a "bad" thought. I was five or six years old. My two sisters and I (a third sister came a couple of years later) were in my parents' bedroom getting ready for bed. I began crying, and I couldn't stop. My parents were worried and asked why I was so upset. After gasping and gulping for several minutes, I blurted out: "I thought that God is a pig." A fairly benign image, but at the time it was the nastiest one I could come up with. I was convinced I would be punished for it. My parents were immediately relieved that I wasn't holding in some more debilitating trauma. They tried to comfort me: it's all right; God isn't a pig; don't worry about your thought.

But I did. For years. Bad thoughts weren't good. Decades later I was able to see that my bad thought was really about my biological father, who had an unpredictable temper and who was closer to and more active with me than God was. At that young age, I couldn't bring myself to say or think that my dad was a pig, so it was safer to project the bad thought onto my Heavenly Father. Which scared me even more. Over time I have learned to pay more attention to God's grace and mercy, but the images and messages of God's vengeance that framed much of my childhood can still bubble up to haunt me.

The billboard by the Lincoln Tunnel reinforced the notion of a fierce and calculating God. Psychic safety is a primordial need, so I can understand the desire to keep a vengeful God up in heaven rather than here with us. If we can keep our noses clean, it is safe to say that God will stay there. Don't make him come down here.

Like many of us, the first prayer I learned was the Lord's Prayer. Its familiarity makes it feel intimate, but the location of God is distant: "Our Father, who art in heaven." For theologian Thomas Berry, the Lord's Prayer suggests that God is an absentee landlord. "We are in trouble," I remember Berry saying, "when we begin the Lord's Prayer, 'Our Father, who art in heaven,' it means that we locate God up there, which of course is not here. This means that we can exercise dominion over the earth." This is, he pointed out, what we have done to an incredibly destructive degree. And God has not yet come down to punish our ecological malfeasance.

The converse of a distant God is a divine presence who is everywhere. For several years in my twenties and thirties, I found this idea comforting; the notion of a loving presence provided an important corrective to the distant disciplinarian who continued to invade my psyche. Yet after a while the concept of the ubiquity of God became problematic because it felt too vague; instead of enhancing God's presence and power, it reduced it. I wanted to be with God, but I needed a location for God—not for God's sake, but for mine. I couldn't get my head or my prayer around a God who is everywhere. God seemed too diffuse, too uninvolved. In a rather bizarre paradox, I found that if God was everywhere, the idea was so global that I couldn't find God anywhere. It was too hard to pay attention to a God I couldn't locate in space and time. Years later, I would wrestle with the paradox of God being everywhere and nowhere, but not in my older childhood and young adulthood. I began to pay attention to situations and places where I could best be with God and where God could best be with me.

It started with church. I was taught that church was God's house, and my family entered that house on a weekly basis, with respect and reverence. The space, and especially the music, suggested to me that God was there. I felt drawn into the space and the liturgy, because at a subliminal level I felt I was being drawn into God. I had some ambivalence about this, especially in my early years, because showing respect in God's house meant dressing up. I didn't mind the tie so much, but I literally chafed at the gray flannel pants I had to wear. This was especially problematic on the monthly Sundays when there was Communion. The service lasted longer than the other weekly services, and we had to kneel for most of it. I can still feel the itch from my pants, which was relieved somewhat when I discovered the unexpected balm of long underwear.

Despite my physical discomfort, I found myself drawn into the mystery of the ritual. As a ten-year-old, the words, movements, and symbolic actions were baffling to me, but beneath it all I could sense that something important and powerful was happening. Even though I didn't understand what was going on, I felt the need to be there, because I was being fed in some strange and wonderful way. I was being blessed by a God who was somehow present in that space.

Many years later, as a seminarian, I immersed myself in the history and purpose of liturgy. It provided an important academic context for my understanding of the Eucharist, which in the mid-1970s was becoming the primary worship offering in the Episcopal Church. But it was only when I heard a presentation on the spiritual and psychic dynamics of the Eucharist that I was able to more freely and deeply experience its impact. As a good friend of mine said to me years ago, "God is easy to experience, but difficult to understand." He went on to say that for the most part, the Christian church has reversed that truth, by portraying God as easy to understand but difficult to experience. In that way, the church has held dominion over people's understanding, and limited, if not controlled, their experience. It has exercised that dominion repeatedly over the centuries; when individual experiences of God have not fit the prevailing theological framework, the church has often responded harshly, if not cruelly.

That historical legacy of orthodoxy (right belief), along with an intellectual pressure to understand the Eucharist, had shrouded my opportunity to experience it. As I look back over my participation in church life, however, I have always been drawn to the experience of being with God, even though I may not have been able to name it.

I had a taste of that experience as a young boy, but no real framework for sustaining it. The framework that I absorbed during seminary and carry with me now is the symbolic presentation of two intersecting journeys—of Jesus and of the rest of us. Jesus has taken the journey, and we are invited to go along with him. It is a journey beneath history and beyond our cognitive understanding. It is a journey into mystery that we are invited to experience.

In the fifth century, St. Augustine declared that if we want to ascend to God, we must first descend with him. The narrative in the eucharistic service describes the descent of Jesus of Nazareth as he approaches the crucifixion. Jesus's descent parallels our own—into vulnerability, fear, disappointment, and depression, conditions that are inevitable parts of life. The culmination of the Eucharist occurs when the bread is broken at the altar by the priest. It symbolizes Jesus's broken body, and at the same time it symbolizes our own brokenness.

After Jesus's and our journeys intersect, an amazing exchange takes place. We are invited to come forward and receive what has been blessed on the altar. When we come forward, we bring all our brokenness, all the bad thoughts, resentments, hurts, and losses that we have accumulated on our journey, aware of them or not—and we leave them at the altar. In return, we take a piece of bread and a sip of wine. It is Jesus's life, broken for anyone and everyone who comes to receive it. It is new life for us that can fill and transform. Yet the brokenness of life continues to seep into our bones and souls and weighs us down. So we come back again and again—bringing our hurts and the parts of our lives that are, in fact, of death—and taking back hope.

To the uninitiated, the skeptic, or the fierce unbeliever, this weekly presentation of bread and wine at the altar, and the parade of people who line up to receive it, can seem like an antiquated ritual that has long since lost its meaning. The reverence of the priest who celebrates the ritual on the altar and of the people who come to receive the bread and wine at the altar rail may seem sincere, but to an increasingly secular world, the reverence can also seem misplaced, if not silly.

I experience God in the mystery of the ritual. Words cannot adequately carry the freight of the mystery, but symbols can, particularly if the symbols, narrative, adornments, music, and movements are arranged carefully as an invitation into the experience of the mystery. The mystery can move our souls to sense God's presence.

I would like to be able to say that my soul is always lifted by this regular exchange of bringing my psychic and spiritual brokenness to the altar and receiving the mysterious presence of God in the bread and wine—that I always experience the gift of new life. But there are times when I am too distracted or depressed, or I have fashioned the delusion that I am not broken. Or I just don't believe it. Or I get wrapped up in the work of an internal liturgical review committee that I have appointed myself to, critiquing the sequence or the movements or the music. Still, there are enough times when I am humble and vulnerable enough to experience God's presence in the bread and wine that I continue to participate in this ritual with expectation and longing. Over the years I have told people that receiving the Eucharist is the most important thing that I do in my life, because it enables me to do everything else. That may be slightly hyperbolic, but not by much. The symbolic infusion of new life mysteriously present in the Eucharist keeps me going. The sacrament of the Eucharist is a ritual where God reliably shows up, for me anyway. It is in the bread and wine that I can locate and experience God's presence.

When the COVID-19 pandemic hit in early 2020, receiving Communion was, in most Episcopal churches, shut down. The presence of

God, at least the symbolic location of God, was taken away. For so many, this was disorienting, if not debilitating. Where did God go?

After months of not receiving Communion, I began to realize that my devotion to the Eucharist had a shadow side: I was unintentionally limiting God's presence to a space and a ritual. It was the opposite of God being everywhere. The intersection of the two journeys and the symbolic exchange of giving over that which is of death and then receiving life were integral components to my spiritual health, but limited my sense of God's location and the potential to experience God in other situations.

I was not alone. In the first weeks of the COVID shutdown, debates raged on and on among many church folks about whether or not people could put bread and wine in front of a computer screen and consider it blessed by a priest who was performing a livestreamed Eucharist. Was it legitimate? There were some clear theological and liturgical issues to sort through, but it seemed to me that a deeper dynamic was in play: if the reliability of God's showing up was in question, where could we now locate God? The Eucharist had traditionally demonstrated to so many of us that God is not only close, but we can ingest God's presence (unlike the God who resides beyond the stratosphere and comes down only when we screw up). That had now been taken away, so where did God go?

God was, and is, reliably present and at work elsewhere. Just as close, but harder to see because my attention had been trained to focus on God in the sacred places—in church, at the altar, in disciplined prayer. The COVID crisis generated no end of anxiety and confusion for me, as for many others. Working through that (which wasn't easy), however, revealed a paradox: as things shut down, the opportunity to see God at work opened up.

God was—and is—close. I drew on the testimony of St. Benedict, the founder of Western monasticism, who remarked that we can see the face of God in someone else. COVID presented some challenges to the approach implied by Benedict's witness, given that most people's faces were shrouded by masks. In a group discussion with parish leaders, we lamented that we couldn't see people smile through their masks. One woman offered that she had learned to see people smiling with their eyes. Her comment shifted the conversation for the rest of us and gave me an opportunity to locate God's presence in a new way.

God is close. I have been learning to train a spiritual muscle to locate God in nearness. There are sacramental moments that occur regularly, in the everyday. When I focus on someone's smile, greeting, or invitation to recognize goodness and wholeness, my anxiety, confusion, and distraction are mysteriously replaced by the gift of life.

After receiving the Eucharist, and being fed with a taste of new life, we are then sent out: "Go in peace to love and serve the Lord." The feeding, the new life, has a purpose: do God's work. In each encounter with a person or situation that enables me to locate God's presence, there is also an invitation, no less compelling: Join God in doing God's work. Be with God, yes, but work with God to heal, bless, and guide.

There is a sacramental quality to all of this, and the pandemic shutdown has opened me up to it, enabling me to more deeply appreciate the instruction Jesus gives to his disciples: "and whoever gives even a cup of cold water to one of these little ones in the name of a disciple—truly I tell you, none of these will lose their reward" (Matthew 10:42).

The reward is in joining God. Giving a cup of water, serving a meal, greeting the stranger, offering hospitality—these are holy acts, because in those moments God is present. We are joining with a God who is not in a distant heaven or hovering on our shoulder ready to wreak vengeance but is in the midst of the encounter—offering blessing and peace, and exposing injustice.

These moments of blessing can occur when we least expect it. Several years ago, it came time for my wife and me to put down our beloved fourteen-year-old dog, Katie. She couldn't walk or eat, and it was clear that she was in a lot of pain. When we got to the animal hospital and brought her out of the car, a woman we didn't know was coming out of the office with her pet. She immediately understood why we were there, and with a reverence and grace that I will never forget, she held open the door. It was an amazingly tender act of hospitality. It softened the pain that we were feeling and in some mysterious way prepared us for what was next. It wasn't until much later that I was able to reflect that God was at work in the silent compassion of an anonymous stranger. I could have missed it; after all, she was just showing us the courtesy of opening the door. On one level, she was being polite. On another, her kindness opened a window into God's presence.

I began this chapter by asking the question, Where is God? What I have learned is that is the wrong question to ask, because although it enables us to attempt to locate God—at a distance or everywhere or someplace in between—the question does not imply a relationship. The question we need to wrestle with is, Where is God working? Which, of course, presupposes that God is in fact at work, active in healing, guiding, and blessing. Which then leads to another question: How do we join God in God's work?

I have also learned over the years that the more attention I pay to God showing up, the more God shows up. And the invitation to join God becomes more compelling, if not urgent. Paying attention to God is a spiritual muscle that we can strengthen and develop.

Yet, how often do we consider that spiritual muscle superfluous? If we believe in the existence of a remote, distant, and uninvolved God, it leaves us to take charge ourselves. Writer and teacher Parker Palmer calls this "functional atheism." A functional atheist is someone who says they believe in God, but lives as though God doesn't exist. To them, God is a concept, not a presence. A functional atheist embraces the idea of God and can accept the existence of God, but cannot imagine that God is working in the world or in one's life. It can feel too risky, or too foolish, to think that the presence of God is somehow engaged in the world. So we end up trying to manage everything ourselves.

I confess that I am a recovering functional atheist. I often tell myself that I have enough intelligence, energy, humility, and electronic devices that I can get through life on my own. I offer silence, worship, and lip service to God, but when life gets difficult, I insist on trying to sort things through by myself. In those self-absorbed moments it really doesn't matter where God is, or even *if* God is. I become the sole steward of my own destiny, an attitude that gets no end of support in our ego-driven culture, which puts the individual front and center and is relentlessly focused on instant gratification. Besides, my self-absorbed thinking goes, God is busy. God has to worry about the economy, gun violence, climate change, and God knows what else, so *I* will give God a break. It's an act of charity on my part. My agenda doesn't hold a candle to God's. Whenever I fall into this mindset, which happens more often than I care to admit or recognize, I get in trouble—because I have become disconnected from my true self.

We can argue whether or not this disconnection is sin or alienation; however we describe it, it is very real; and has long been an issue in the human family, particularly in the Christian-dominated West. It shows up in scripture, when some confused followers of Jesus seek a quick and easy exit from their distress. "Sir, we wish to see Jesus" (John 12:21), some Greeks ask Philip at the Passover festival. They want to be connected to him in a clear and unambiguous way. I know that desire. Having Jesus show up when I want him to show up, so that I can easily see him, will cure me of my functional atheism—or so I tell myself. Doubt will then disappear. Jesus will take over. In the story, the Greeks' request is passed up the chain of command to Jesus, who offers a rather cryptic response: "Those who love their life lose it, and those who hate their life in this world will keep it for eternal life" (John 12:25). In effect, Jesus is saying that we need to develop a spiritual muscle, which will help us see in a way that is different from the way the world sees. Jesus will be present—not as an overseer or a magician, but as a partner. Lose the way of the world; let go of the culturally reinforced attachment to self-reliance so you can love life more. Become free of the ubiquitous instant gratification model, which runs the culture and drives the ego. Together, these changes are the antidote to functional atheism.

This will take practice and support from others—and a willingness to engage in a process of discernment. To sit with the questions and options. To wrestle internally with the confusion. To be willing to lose our hardened ideas and perceptions (which often govern our life)—and to be open to a new life. It takes time. It takes practice. And it requires help—from God and from one another. The discipline of discernment is part of our spiritual muscle training; without it we won't notice God's presence in all the places where God is working, or be able to join God there. Because we will be in our own way—with our unfed or defeated egos, or with our culturally trained need for instant gratification. To say God *is* everywhere is a bit of a dodge; but to say that God is *working* everywhere is an invitation to see God at work and to join God in that work. As we train our spiritual muscle to see God at work, not only in the big moments but also and particularly in the small ones, we become better able to join our passion with God's presence.

And by joining God in God's ongoing work, we can make a difference—in ourselves and in the world.

THE HOSPITALITY OF JESUS

We know from the gospels that Jesus taught. From those same sources we know that Jesus prayed, healed, and, according to various stories, performed miracles. But perhaps more than all the dramatic teachings, healings, and miracles, Jesus spent his time simply being with others, be they his disciples, his followers, tax collectors, sinners, demoniacs, women, or prostitutes. Except for religious and civic power brokers, whom he challenged and chastised, Jesus sat with people, ate with people (including those who cultural and religious norms determined shouldn't be at the table), traveled with people, and stayed overnight with people, whether friends, family, or strangers.

One of the most compelling stories for me of Jesus being with people is recounted in Luke 24. The story takes place on Easter Day, when two followers of Jesus, Simon and Cleopas, are heading to Emmaus, a town seven miles away from Jerusalem. Given the incidents of the past several days, Jerusalem had become too dangerous a place for anyone who had a connection with Jesus. As they walk on the road, the two followers are approached by a stranger. We know he is the risen Christ, but they don't yet know who he is. He asks them, rather coyly, what has been going on (as if he didn't know). They respond rather incredulously: hadn't he heard that their leader had been arrested, tried, tortured, and then crucified? And then that very morning, they go on to say, they had heard from some women who had seen Jesus come back from the dead. This was too much to take in, so they were headed to Emmaus. Anyplace but Jerusalem.

The stranger then asks if he can accompany them on their journey. They agree, and for the rest of the seven miles the stranger regales them with stories of God acting in history. By the time they reach Emmaus, the pair have developed a relationship with this stranger and invite him to be their guest at the inn where they are staying, an invitation that Jesus accepts. Later on, while at dinner, Jesus takes the bread that is offered, blesses and breaks it, and then gives it to them: "Then their eyes were opened, and they recognized him; and he vanished from their sight" (Luke 24:31).

It is a dramatic and life-transforming moment. They recognize the living Christ and go immediately to tell the other disciples that they have seen the risen Lord.

It is a great story, but from nearly every cultural and religious perspective, the story should not have played out the way it is presented in scripture. Since Jesus was the invited guest, when he took up the bread to bless it, his hosts would have said—should have said—"Oh no, you are our guest. Let us bless and break the bread." If they had held to cultural and religious norms, they would not have come to see the risen Christ. They allowed the guest to become the host, and their lives were never the same.

Norms of behavior, traditional expectations, and undifferentiated anxiety can dull our ability to see. And given our cultural (Cartesian) priority on thinking, we can go through much of our lives so laser-focused on the task at hand that our eyes are essentially closed to anything on the periphery.

Years ago, I was in a two-day preaching workshop with a group of colleagues. We had agreed that on the second day we would have our sermons videotaped, so each of us could see what we looked and sounded like, and hear one another's feedback. My schedule was such that I had a limited time to prepare in my office the night before. Just when I was getting some clarity about what I wanted to say, the doorbell rang. I slammed my fist on the desk, cursed into the silence, and headed to the door. Without opening it, I knew who would be on the other side—yet another homeless person looking for midnight mercy. I didn't want to provide it. I had work to do.

My predictions were confirmed when I opened the door: there stood a homeless young man. But he seemed different from other shelter seekers who came by late at night. He stood some distance from the door. He looked humble, although, I thought, that could be part of his con. It was immediately clear that he wasn't drunk or high. I didn't take this as good news, because I felt compelled to allow him in. In halting English, he said he needed a place to stay, and with some graciousness he asked if I could help. I went back into my office and called the local shelter. They had a bed available, and he was welcome to it.

This meant I needed to drive him there. My duty to this man was wrapped up in constricting resentment. I was an intensely reluctant host. I fairly shoved him in the car and started to drive the five minutes to the shelter. At a stoplight, I thought I should at least find out something about him. "Where are you from?" I asked.

"Nicaragua," he replied. Since this was during the Nicaraguan civil war, I asked him if he was one of the Sandinistas, who made up the rebel forces. "No, no," he said, shaking his head. Was he one of the Contras, who were on the other side of the conflict? "No, no," he said as he shook his head again. "I am a Christian." His response was not so much a description, but a conviction. It came from a very deep place—and only when he identified his faith was I able, or willing, to really look at him. The intensity and graciousness of his manner evoked a similar response in me. His humility was genuine, as was his courage—and it melted away my task-driven obsessiveness so I could see him more fully, something I hadn't wanted to do until that moment. He became my host. His name was Santos Garcia, and he was fleeing conflict and having a hard time figuring out what to do next.

I dropped him off at the shelter, where he thanked me and we said goodbye. I never saw him again, but the memory of the encounter lingers as a moment of grace and as a warning to pay attention to where and how God shows up: to resist the temptation to see the other in a certain and limited way, precluding any real opportunity for relationship.

For the past four hundred and fifty years or so, in the wealthy Christian West (relative to much of the rest of the world), the ministry and mission of the Church has been largely focused on "doing for" others. The Church, through almsgiving and systems of disbursement, has provided food, shelter, clothing—basic life necessities. That is important and, indeed, necessary. If people don't have food, we are compelled by Jesus's teaching to give them something to eat. If people have no place to stay, we need to provide shelter. But the possible (unintentional) consequence of this centuries-old model of ministry is that it may reinforce the gap between giver and receiver. The host remains as host, and the guest is expected to be a grateful recipient. This is a transaction rather than a relationship.

People who serve meals to the hungry on Thanksgiving and Christmas may go home feeling good about their act of mercy, but without having had much more than a brief exchange with those they have served, often come away with reinforced projections of what it is to be poor. Conversely, people who receive the hospitality of the servers often go away with a reinforced projection of what it is to be rich. In both cases, distance is maintained and relationships are limited to the transactional. Allowing the guest to become the host, reflects a commitment that everyone has something to offer and creates an environment in which individuals may move back and forth between these roles, mitigating the status ascribed to one role or the other. That reciprocity allows us to fully see one another. It offers the opportunity to learn from those who seem most different from us, transforming our lives in new and unexpected ways. Seeing deeply involves risk; it may require some breach of norms. Jesus broke those norms nearly every day, even after the resurrection.

The Emmaus story provides a window into Jesus's hospitality. Jesus meets Simon and Cleopas where they are, in the middle of their escape to Emmaus. They are not able to recognize Jesus because they are so wrapped up in their fear, anxiety, and cultural expectation. Jesus doesn't confront them. Instead, he walks with them, he listens to them, trusting that his hospitality of invitation will generate a similar response in them. Thanks to Jesus's ongoing hospitality throughout their seven-mile sojourn, Simon and Cleopas are able to move through their fear and anxiety, and reciprocate Jesus's hospitality by allowing him to be the host.

As a result of this reciprocal hospitality, the disciples see Jesus and are transformed.

I imagine that Simon and Cleopas were distraught and confused when Jesus met them on the road to Emmaus. They had witnessed a crucifixion; their grief over the loss of their leader was disabling and disorienting—they must have feared they would be next to be nailed to a cross. It took seven miles and several hours for them to be open to the hospitality of a stranger.

Most everyone in America was distraught and confused on September 11, 2001. I was meeting with a church leader when a staff member interrupted us to say that a plane had flown into the World Trade Center. I presumed it was a twin-engine two-seater (which had happened in New York a few years earlier). Minutes later, in a phone call with a diocesan leader, I learned it was a commercial airliner. The leader was in tears because her daughter was flying that morning. She called back a few minutes later to report that her daughter was safe. The parish nurse then came into my office and said she was nervous because her daughter was flying from Boston to Los Angeles. Thinking she was unnecessarily upset, I began to make plans for our weekly staff meeting. Seeing her anxiety, rarely on display, the other priest on staff asked if he could drive her home, and she readily agreed. Irritated that my morning plans were being interrupted and supposing her fears would come to naught, I agreed to drive her home instead. I didn't want to be accused of a lack of compassion, even though at that moment I didn't feel any.

When we got to her house, we met her husband, who had been watching TV as the first tower came down. About an hour later they received a phone call from her daughter's company that she had been on the first plane to hit the towers.

I went into problem-solving mode, seeking ways to care for the situation. I attempted to comfort the family, but I was more focused on what I needed to do next. I called back to the office to make plans for the congregation to host a community prayer service that evening. I called my wife to see if our kids, who were at different high schools, were okay. They were.

All my actions were efforts to avoid the pain of what was going on—with this family and across the world.

It can feel safer to hold on to the role of host.

Jesus knew of Simon and Cleopas's need to escape, and he knows of ours—and of our need to serve as host in uncomfortable situations in order to maintain our illusion of control. Jesus will wait, he will walk with us, and he will listen. Long enough so that maybe, just maybe, we can turn the tables and allow the guest to be the host. When we can allow those we feel compelled to serve to offer their gifts to us in reciprocity, both parties are offered greater possibilities for personal and cultural transformation.

This can be hard to do. Even when we have a clear sense of our mission, our intention can create a kind of tunnel vision, such that we are unable to see anything beyond the framework of our purpose. I was six months into my tenure as rector of All Saints Church in Worcester, Massachusetts, in 1993 when there was a shooting in the neighborhood. A person was killed in a drug deal gone bad. A group of parish leaders gathered the next day, and we pondered how we should respond. After some discernment, we decided to offer what we do best, which was our liturgy. So we designed a procession of hope, which involved prayers, litanies, songs, and the sprinkling of water to restore the ground that had been violated through violence. We invited people to join us on a procession through the neighborhood on a Sunday afternoon. People came—from the parish and from the immediate, recently gentrified, neighborhood.

There was a profound sense of healing in what we did. People felt relieved and hopeful, and so we decided to hold the procession again. A local synagogue asked if they could join us. We readily agreed and set out on another Sunday afternoon.

We went through the gentrified neighborhood (where the shooting had taken place), and then we began to walk down the hill. The residents in the adjacent neighborhood had skin of different tones and spoke a different language. We didn't know them, and they didn't know us. The procession, led by a cross and a Star of David, with women clergy, made sense in the gentrified neighborhood, but it felt disconnected as we moved away from the familiar. We knew the people on top of the hill, but I was embarrassed to admit that I knew next to nothing about the stories and circumstances of the people who lived one block down. I really hadn't seen them.

We discontinued the procession and decided that we needed to learn about the neighborhood. A group of us began a rhythm of walking the area on a weekly basis when the weather turned warm. We stopped to talk with people who were sitting outside. Our intent was to listen, but in our initial encounters we did a lot of talking, mainly because of our anxiety as we literally stepped outside of what we knew. We asked people if they knew our All Saints Church, the large church a couple blocks up the hill. Most didn't know the church until they realized that it was the building that had hosted a Head Start program for the past thirty years. Many of their kids had been in the program, as had some of the parents. Occasionally, we all had trouble with the confusion of sorting through English and Spanish, but if we listened long enough and dared to get beyond anxiety and stereotypes to simply be with one another, relationships began to build. And we could see one another more fully.

Sort of.

Neighborhood kids began attending an after-school ministry at the church. Through them, a level of trust began to develop with some of the parents. A couple of kids attended church every now and then. In my excitement, I asked a mother if her boys, ages nine and eleven, would be interested in joining the Men and Boys Choir. The mother was willing, the boys seemed eager, and I spoke with the music director, who was ready to engage them in the training program.

I got the boys to their first rehearsal, in a room in the church they had never in been before and for a program for which they had no context. I thought we were behaving as gracious hosts. I expected them to see the choir as a real opportunity, but I had laid very little groundwork for the mother and her sons. My desire to be "host" precluded my paying attention to any of their concerns. I imagined that their participation would be the first step in getting neighborhood kids in our choir, which would further diversify the congregation and its long and lauded musical history. That was my agenda. I would look and feel good. I did not notice any concerns they brought or confusion they might have. And if I had really paid attention, I would have noticed that the brothers looked uncomfortable. They knew me, but didn't really know the space or what was expected—or what they were in for. I hadn't really thought through what gifts they might be bringing; and how they might have the opportunity to teach something to me or to the music program. I saw hosting as my job, and I was anchored in managing a program of assistance for the family I saw as in need of our help. It wasn't enough. The boys didn't come back. We hadn't created the space or established a relationship for them to feel comfortable.

3

BEING WITH

W hen I began my ministry as bishop of the Diocese of Newark in early 2007, I noticed the soup line that gathered outside the Roman Catholic church located immediately next door to our four-story building downtown. We shared a driveway and a gate, which the diocese technically owned and kept locked, requiring those seeking a meal to walk around the block to get to the soup line. Good fences make good neighbors, as the poet Robert Frost wrote. And we were good neighbors, in the sense that we had no relationship with one another. We didn't pay attention to them, and they didn't bother us. The locked gate made sure of that. I did notice that there were a lot of men who arrived twice a day and ate outside — always outside. And I learned that the church was not used except for a weekly service for the deaf and a mass on Ash Wednesday.

And then, after a few weeks, I no longer noticed the men, the Catholic church, or the gate. It all became an urban foreground for the Passaic River, which flowed just beyond the church and captured the eye's attention (if one was looking at all). Those men were poor, and to me at that time they were faceless, nameless—and story-less. They were a local cohort of "the poor," which didn't exactly mean that they were untouchable as a caste and therefore consigned to societal rejection, but it was culturally permissible to avoid them. And so I did.

I told myself that I needed to do so, because as I became more acclimated to my new role, my gaze and attention were directed at the one hundred plus congregations in the diocese—to their clergy and laypeople, their problems, and their opportunities. Lots of things were happening. There was a lot to see and an enormous amount to learn. I couldn't, or wouldn't, see anything else. When I arrived at the office in the morning, our parking lot, located against the fence and near the gate, was for me no more than a parking lot. There were people eating breakfast on the other side—but I literally didn't see them.

Several years into my ministry, a priest in the diocese asked what was going on next door. I told her there was a feeding program at breakfast and lunch. "Let's go," she said, and a group of us went through the gate to the other side—not to serve, but to talk with some of the men, many of whom had been coming daily for years. I learned from the two permanent staff members of the feeding program, whom I hadn't met before, that they averaged five hundred people a day, mostly men (a relatively small number of women ate inside, in the church rectory)—two hundred fifty in the morning and an equal number at noon. And I hadn't seen them. All I knew is that they were poor.

Afterward, when our group gathered to reflect on what we'd seen, heard, and learned, the priest who had initially asked about the soup line pointed a finger at me and said rather forcefully, "Don't you dare go just once."

And I didn't. I made it a point of going at least weekly—to talk, and more importantly, to listen. Almost everyone who came to the soup kitchen had been sidelined at some point in their life, some by their own actions or by illness, but many because of a system that denied, diminished, or dismissed them (almost everyone was Black or Hispanic). There was a fair amount of turnover in those who came to eat, but many were regulars, and with some I was able to develop a relationship. And the more I went and listened, the more I learned. I heard stories of tragedy and abandonment, of loss and disappointment. At the same time, I heard expressions of hope and graciousness. And I learned that many of these men had lived with a level of courage and faith that I had never had to match in my own life. Many of them became my teachers. Over time they were less defined by the catch-all term of "the poor" and more identified by their individual lives and stories.

Over the years I developed a particularly close relationship with Al, a soup line regular. We often shared what we had been reading. He told me he was reading James Joyce. I was rather skeptical, and said so: "Hardly anyone reads James Joyce, because nobody can understand James Joyce." (I could never get through his novels.) But Al said not only was he reading James Joyce, but he was enjoying it. He then asked me what I was reading, and I told him I was reading *Between the World and Me* by Ta-Nehisi Coates, which had just been published (2015). I told him that Coates maintains that the American dream is designed for people like me (white) at the expense of people like Al (Black). He looked at me quizzically and said, "You didn't know that?" I did know that, but not to the extent and depth that Al did.

Over the course of time, there was a movement from being strangers to becoming neighbors. Early on we unlocked the gate so those who came to eat had easier access. Some members of the diocesan staff went over once a month to serve lunch. Yet it needs to be said that some staff members had a harder time with the transition—some guests would wander over to our side and eat next to the diocesan entrance or leave food on someone's car or occasionally interact with people coming in and out of our building in less than gracious ways. We established some guidelines with the staff members next door (who after a time became important friends), but it wasn't always a smooth transition.

And there was another movement, which was more subtle and perhaps more profound, from having no relationship at all with our neighbors to *being with* them. Being with—which is both an invitation and a struggle. It certainly was a struggle for me. It seemed more natural to me at the time to keep a distance. Serve up a meal, feel good about it, and return my attention to my diocesan ministry, which was all-consuming and supposed to be my primary focus. The lingering messages from our wealthy Western culture, my privileged background, and my rather lofty ecclesiastical role had subliminally taught me that I didn't need to be *with* these neighbors. Or shouldn't be with them. Do for them, maybe, and then move on. Keep them as *them*: the anonymous and story-less poor.

That would have been a great loss.

When Jesus is asked by a lawyer, "Who is my neighbor?" he responds with the parable of the Good Samaritan (Luke 10:29–37). For me, and probably for most of us, the focus of the story has long been on the Samaritan, whose care for a man lying on the side of the Jericho road after a brutal mugging has been held up as a model of what it means to be a neighbor—"go and do likewise" (Luke 10:37). The Samaritan "did for" the wounded man in a compassionate and self-sacrificing way, as opposed to the priest and Levite who did nothing—they just walked by.

But the Samaritan didn't just provide care and charity for the wounded man. He paid the innkeeper to take care of the wounded man while he continued on his journey. And then the Samaritan said to the innkeeper, "and when I come back, I will repay you whatever more you spend" (Luke 10:35). *And when I come back.* The Samaritan's ministry was more than a moment in time. The implication was that he would come back to continue his ministry and in so doing will perhaps build a relationship so that each man can learn from the other.

It was not always easy to fit my visits next door into the rhythm of my life. There were times when I was traveling or on vacation. For three months I was on sabbatical. I had meetings. There were weeks when I couldn't fit it in. There were times I did go, but made such a quick sweep of the soup line that I don't think anyone noticed I was there. Al wasn't around. Nor were Charlie or Pedro or some of the others I often talked to. I didn't try and stop to talk to anyone else. I told myself I didn't have enough time, but what was really going on was that I didn't want to. On those occasions there was no *being with*, but I did feel some satisfaction that I had at least made an effort, and I supposed that counted for something.

But counting is not the measure of ministry, although you wouldn't know it given the emphasis the church places on metrics, numbers, and dollars. My quick trip satisfied some unofficial metric matrix that I kept in my mind. On one level, my non-relational visits were acts of righteousness. After all, I had gone next door into a unique mission field. And people who had never been next door, many of whom would never even consider going next door, were impressed. People like righteousness, myself included. And it feels good to impress people. For centuries we have been conditioned to *do for* as the model of mission; and righteousness continues to be a foundational ingredient in doing for. Mission based in righteousness ends up being more about "us"—and less about "them." It creates a division, which might be intentional, but more often is not. When we offer mission from the perspective of righteousness, we run the risk of becoming agents intent on making an impression—on ourselves. And it reinforces the gap between those who serve and those being served.

The invitation to *be with* is a struggle—but also a gift. I hope to highlight some of Jesus's invitations—his invitations to drill down into the struggles to be with others, with God, or with political or ideological differences. The gift happens when there is transformation, when *being with* is mutual, trusting, and open, and the beloved community becomes manifest.

It turns out that Jesus had a lot to say about the poor. He spoke to them, he spoke of them—and often invited them to eat with him, breaking all sorts of social and religious conventions. And at the same time Jesus was challenging nearly everyone who was not poor to do something to correct the situation. Jesus tells the rich man seeking eternal life that he lacks one thing: he needs to sell all his possessions and give the money to the poor (Luke 18:22). At another point, he tells the story of a wealthy man who hosts a banquet but all of his invited guests beg off, so he invites the poor (Luke 14:13). Jesus demonstrates consistent and compassionate concern for the poor.

But.

"The poor" don't have names, and they don't have stories. All they have is a category—the poor. They remain anonymous, which invites our projections and over the centuries has generated disdain.

When John the Baptist is locked up in prison and word gets back to Jesus that John is wondering if his ministry proclaiming Jesus as the Messiah is all for naught, Jesus responds, "Tell John what you see and hear: the blind receive their sight, the lame walk, the deaf hear, those who have leprosy are cured, the dead are raised—and the poor have good news preached to them" (Luke 7:22). Jesus identifies people by categories, but in each category people are restored to wholeness: they are no longer blind or lame or deaf—or dead. They are changed.

Not so with "the poor." They have good news preached to them, and while we can assume that the good news will bring about some change, Jesus doesn't identify what that change will be. Over and over again, Jesus demonstrated that he could heal individual people. That he could restore their bodies. But to heal an oppressive economic system was not in his purview. It was far too complex, entrenched, and impersonal. He couldn't very well lay hands on the economy or make a paste with dirt and spit and apply it to the marketplace, as he did with the blind man (John 9:6). Jesus knew that. He regularly preached against injustice and called out those whose wealth was achieved through the oppression of others. He could do all that, but he couldn't heal the system. So in his language, when it came to people who were poor, he identified them as casualties of an unjust economic structure. Despite Jesus's teaching, we have continued to lump people who are poor into an economic category without names or stories. A growing number of scholars maintain that Jesus sought to set up alternative communities of equality, particularly in terms of economic resources, where people could freely and fully be with one another. When Jesus included "give us this day our daily bread" in the Lord's Prayer, he was arguing that the 50–70 percent of people living in Roman-occupied Israel who struggled with hunger should be adequately, if not abundantly, fed.

When we are able to move beyond placing people in categories like "the poor," we see people as individuals and are more inclined to be with one another in a more reciprocal way. When I was in college in the early 1970s, Bill Russell came to speak to the student body in a public lecture. He had recently retired from the Boston Celtics, where he led the team to eleven National Basketball Association championships in his thirteen-year career. He is widely considered to be one of the ten best basketball players of all time. While he was imposing in size (6 feet 10 inches tall), he was more impressive in dignity. He talked a bit about basketball, but mostly he shared his considerable wisdom. He refused to be categorized. He told a story of a woman who came up to him at an airport, and said, "Oh, you're a basketball player." He quickly and gently corrected her: "No, ma'am, I am a man who plays basketball." His humanity came first. Throughout his life he has insisted that people recognize both his humanity and the humanity of one another, and not see ourselves as part of some category. There was breadth and depth to his person, and he challenged people to recognize that. The way language was used made a difference.

For centuries, we have been biblically and culturally socialized into lumping poor people into an amorphous economic category: the poor. The term reinforces distance between "the poor" and everybody else, and subliminally maintains the gap between those who have financial security and those who don't. And it prevents us from being with one another.

Ever since hearing Bill Russell nearly fifty years ago, I have tried to avoid use of "the poor" and instead describe people as financially or economically poor. I make this linguistic change because it narrows the gap between those who have more money and those who have less; it puts humanity first. In his sermon on the mount, Jesus introduces a descriptor when he blesses the poor in spirit (Matthew 5:3). The term puts some flesh of humanity on the bones of poverty, given that a poverty of spirit is a category that nearly everyone has experienced. There is a thread of connection between those who lack financial resources and those who know what it means to be emotionally impoverished or spiritually empty. It was that thread of connection that kept drawing me back to the men in the soup line next door, and that same thread was tugging at me to establish relationships marked by being with. We need to identify that connection and build on it, especially for people whose lives are lived in various privileged sanctuaries—and who know poverty only as a theoretical construct.

In recent years, I have heard fewer references to "the poor" and more to the "underprivileged," especially when it comes to children. Programs, donations, bus trips, and free tickets are often being offered to underprivileged kids. They are charitable and welcome gestures, and givers respond to the many requests they receive by doing for; but the term still leaves the underprivileged without names or stories. At some level the term recognizes that an economic system that has underprivileged people in it is not a level playing field, because it leaves whole cohorts of people under-resourced, undereducated, and under-accepted. As far as I am concerned, the term "underprivileged" is a linguistic cosmetic that seeks to soften economic and other inequities, but keeps people distant from one another and undermines opportunities for being with.

When I lived in Japan for two years after college, I quickly learned that non-Japanese people were often called *gaijin*, which means outsider. *Gaijin* were people who didn't belong in the very homogeneous Japanese society. The more I heard it—especially when I was called *gaijin* (which often happened in rural and less cosmopolitan areas), the more I resented it. It precluded my having a name. It placed me in a category that—for the people who used the term—I couldn't escape from. Which was exactly the point. The term established and maintained distance between insiders and outsiders. Being called *gaijin* gave me an appreciation of the sting people who are economically poor might feel when they continue to be referred to as "the poor." They are outside—if not literally outside as homeless people, then at least outside the mainstream. And they are not easily let back in. A key difference between my experience as *gaijin* and people who are economically poor is that I knew I would one day leave Japan and would no longer be an outsider. That is not the case with people who are financially poor. A change of address does not automatically change economic status, because they typically move (and move frequently) from one maligned neighborhood to another.

In Matthew 26:11, Jesus says the poor will always be with us. Some make the case that Jesus is endorsing a system and culture that results in a permanent class of "the poor." And the most that people of means can do is to "do for" them: offer charity, compassion, and blessing, but maintain the gap between the poor and everyone else, because Jesus meant for it to be that way. Others indicate that Jesus is making the case that followers of Jesus should do all they can to not only lift people out of poverty, but to correct an unjust economic system that causes it. No doubt Jesus is referring to Deuteronomy 15:11—"since there will never cease to be some in need on the earth"—accompanied with an exhortation that a safety net be designed to prevent people from entering into grinding poverty.

As I reflect on what I feel is a cultural slur by referring to people as "the poor," I am drawn by what I consider to be a hidden message in "the poor will always be with you." Jesus is not making a sociological prediction, but instead is issuing an invitation to be in relationship. Be with one another. The poor will always be with us; we need to be with them—more than benefactors or rescuers or feeders, shelter providers or thrift shop operators. We need to learn from one another. We need to learn to move past concepts into relationships, acknowledging economic difference, yes, but drawing the threads of connection that bind us to one another—poverty of spirit, grief, laughter, hope. When the relationship becomes personal and stories are shared, the categories that serve to maintain distance begin to fall away. Our language then changes— instead of referring to "the poor," we follow Bill Russell's lead by claiming, and seeing, humanity first. And solidarity grows.

PART II

Impediments to Seeing

4

HATE HAS NO HOME HERE

Lawn signs express the commitments, if not the values, of the homeowner. Lawn signs tend to get planted in the weeks before an election, and they are visible exhortations of the owner's political preferences—be it a candidate or a ballot question—for neighbors and for those who drive by. For the most part, the lawn signs are affirmations, and their presence seeks to multiply the affirmation and win votes.

In recent years, there has been a proliferation of HATE HAS No HOME HERE lawn signs across the American landscape. Similar to blatantly political lawn signs (many make the case that HATE HAS No HOME HERE is indeed a subliminal political message), they reflect the owners' commitments and values. Yet the HATE HAS No HOME HERE signs are negative affirmations, in the sense that their presence announces that toxic attitudes are not welcome. Instead of promoting a value or a candidate, the lawn signs are markers of resistance and are meant to be prophylactics against hate. In some sense, they are firewalls against the growing virus of hatred that may be seeking to establish itself in the neighborhood or community.

HATE HAS NO HOME HERE is a sign of renunciation (rejection): that hate has no part of the owner's life and is refused entrance to the owner's home and is embargoed from even walking on the sidewalk.

To think that hate can be banished is a fool's errand, because in my experience, incidents involving hate have intruded into nearly every home. These hate moments are usually fleeting—involving nasty words and, in some cases, violent actions; but like grief, the memory and hurt from these moments can last a long time. The reason TV and movie dramas often feature a teenager yelling "I hate you!" to a parent is because it is a fairly common occurrence. Growing up, I never uttered those words to my parents, but there certainly were times when I thought them.

More often than not, hate is an impulse. It is usually a response to a threat to or an attack on one's self-worth or identity. A privilege is denied, a hurt is applied, intentionally or unintentionally a prejudice is invoked, a person's integrity is unfairly impugned. Without taking any time for thinking or reflection, the wounded person responds in kind— and if the conditions are ripe for escalation, as they often are in a household, verbal or physical spasms of violence can result. Hate shows up, and when it does, it causes damage.

And our ability to see is affected. We literally become shortsighted, in that our energy—and our vision—is focused on the hate we are feeling, expressing, or trying to repress.

HATE HAS NO HOME HERE creates a silo. It announces that hate can't come in, but subliminally it also announces that hate can't get out. Jesus had something to say about this: "Or how can you say to your neighbor, 'Friend, let me take out the speck in your eye,' when you yourself do not see the log in your own eye? You hypocrite, first take the log out of your own eye, and then you will see clearly to take the speck out of your neighbor's eye" (Luke 6:42).

Jesus does not explicitly say that the speck or the log in our eyes is hate, but he is intimating that there are forces—circumstances—that make it difficult to see. I have had a lifelong impediment to seeing that is not emotional, spiritual, or cultural, but genetic: I am color-blind. I am among about ten percent of men (and less than one percent of women) who have inherited a trait that makes it difficult to identify colors. Being color-blind doesn't mean that I can't see colors; but I am rarely able to correctly identify them. I am pretty hopeless when it comes to distinguishing between green and brown. And when it comes to naming what I call the esoteric colors—chartreuse, lavender, peach, coral, teal, Nile green—no way.

Explaining color blindness to the vast majority who are not similarly affected has always been a challenge, and at the same time has made my circumstance an interesting topic of conversation. "So, you don't see colors?" I am often asked. "Yes, I do," I reply, "but I can't always tell you what they are," whereupon an informal test is conducted—someone pointing to my shirt or someone's dress or the wall, "What color is that?" And my response is usually wrong, which provides comedy, along with some intrigue.

I arrived at some self-understanding about my condition when I was in college and read the Phaedo, a chapter in Plato's *Republic*. In it, Socrates asks his students, "How do you know what you know?" And their answer comes back, "Well, we know it because we know it." A facile answer, says Socrates, and not good enough.

How do we know what we know? I have often used Socrates's question on non-color-blind people: "How do you know that the green you identify is green?" I ask. "Because I know it," comes the reply. I press what I think is my Socratic advantage by remarking that they have obviously been trained to recognize green, but they can't really know that it is green (even though light refraction coefficients for differences in colors can be determined which most people can correctly identify—but I don't want to undermine my argument).

In the recent past, the American populace has been deeply engaged in issues of color, on what we see. Since George Floyd's murder in May 2020, there have been a flurry of conversations and demonstrations about race in America. And in response, there has been a significant resistance to the conversations, to the demonstrations—and especially to the succinct and powerful message Black Lives Matter. The resistance often includes people claiming that they are color-blind. The implication is that they don't see difference in the color of people's skin. That everyone is seen to be the same, which means everyone has equal opportunity, privilege, and justice. Because there is no color difference.

I don't buy it.

For centuries the American culture has used distinctions in color to create a hierarchy—a caste system, as author Isabel Wilkerson calls it in her 2020 book, *Caste: The Origins of Our Discontents.* Inevitably the hierarchy leads to hate.

We can't deny the distinctions. We shouldn't be blind to the differences. We need to learn to say that we don't know what we don't know. The challenge—indeed, the opportunity—is to see the distinctions, the differences, not as a problem but as a gift. Claiming racial color blindness is a dodge. It shuts down conversation and impedes us from moving forward. We need help from one another to be able to sort through our confusion, our inability to correctly identify difference—and to guide one another into living in the beloved community.

Hate Has No Home Here is a statement of self-delusion. Hate does exist, both inside and outside. The "log" of hate is opportunistic; it will find a way in, one way or another. And if the intention is to keep hate out, the unintended consequence of claiming that it *Has No Home Here* is to lock in hate's potential, until it is ready to combust.

Hate Has No Home Here is also a statement of misguided self-righteousness: the hater might hate, but the sign owner does not. Whenever I see a Hate Has No Home Here sign, I can't help but think that the owner hates the hater. Which defeats the whole purpose.

Presumably the display of Hate Has No Home Here is a warning to people whose hate has gone beyond impulse to ideology. That the hate that is being exposed and denied has become a way of life for the hater. The hater systemically seeks the denial, diminishment, or destruction of a person or, more likely, a particular group. And the lawn sign says the hate and the hater are not welcome, wanted—or allowed.

I sympathize with this way of thinking, yet there are several problems with it, one of which harks back to what I said about self-righteousness. Everyone I have ever known, including myself, has been taught some degree of prejudice. We either absorbed it at the kitchen table, in the junior high cafeteria, on the playground, or through various TV shows and movies. Or we had prejudice force-fed to us by a bitter family member, a malicious group, or a religious or political stridency that organized itself around hostility. If you think that you've never swallowed this prejudice, overtly or covertly, you need to think again. We all learned it—somehow, somewhere. And we all carry vestiges, sometimes whole chapters, of that prejudice with us. The challenge is to identify the log in our eye, how it got there, and how we can minimize it. So we can see more clearly. To think that we can totally get rid of it is yet another exercise in self-delusion.

And then there is the self-righteousness and self-delusion of the hater. So many people are not aware of their prejudice, and that it can morph into hatred. The seasoned haters, those for whom the lawn signs are intended, are those who are the first to deny that they hate at all. Instead, their commitment to the diminishment, cancellation, and/or destruction of someone else is seen as a mission: clothed in arrogance, functioning in delusion, and reinforced most often by religious ideology. Embedded in denial.

For me, the existence of these ideologues is an assault on my sense of decency, civility, and community. Their hatred threatens the whole idea of virtue. But beneath that, the systematic haters represent an assault on my ego. For me, and for many of us, it is not only that we won't welcome them into our home; we want them gone.

And therein is an even bigger problem. To want them gone, which is an understandable impulse from the ego, carries with it a conviction that they can't be changed. That redemption is just not possible. I remember a class I took in seminary with Henri Nouwen, the incredibly gifted spiritual author and teacher. He said that the greatest sin any of us can ever commit is to hold to the conviction that someone can't be redeemed, that they can't be changed. When that conviction becomes policy, Henri said, you end up with Auschwitz. Foundational to Nazi thinking was that Jews could not be redeemed or changed, which made it easier to develop an elaborate and evil system of systematic murder—a Holocaust.

Expressions and attitudes of hate are a growing problem. They grab us at a visceral level. Our impulse is to respond to hate with hate or to deny its access into our homes or hearts—or to hold on to the conviction that hatred as ideology cannot be changed and therefore needs to be removed or canceled.

None of these responses work. All they do is stir up the hate and scatter it about.

The challenge for people of faith is first to acknowledge our own temptation to hate: to recognize the metaphorical log that resides in every one of our eyes. To be with the hate—to learn how it got there, how it gets triggered and under what circumstances, and how we typically respond to it. More often than not, as noted, hate is a reaction by the ego to an assault on one's self-worth and identity. Hate is always accompanied by anger, be it visible or boiling just beneath the surface. The intensity of the anger (and hate) is usually contingent on the level of threat to the ego. The greater the threat, the more anger and the higher the coefficient of hate.

Jesus met that anger/hate dynamic several times during his ministry, but perhaps no more dramatically than at its beginning and end. Shortly after his forty days in the wilderness, Jesus returns to his hometown synagogue in Nazareth. On the Sabbath, he reads from Isaiah: "The Spirit of the Lord is upon me, because he has anointed me to bring good news to the poor. He has sent me to proclaim release to the captives and recovery of sight to the blind, to let the oppressed go free, to proclaim the year of the Lord's favor" (Luke 4:18–19). The congregation speaks well of him when he gives back the scroll and announces, "Today this scripture has been fulfilled in your hearing" (Luke 4:21). But then their doubts kick in. They are unable to imagine a carpenter's kid having such wisdom.

Jesus challenges their shortsightedness, which enrages the people in the synagogue, who drive him out of town and threaten to hurl him off a cliff. Hospitality turned to anger and boiled into hate.

Three years later Jesus is hailed by a crowd as he rides into the city of Jerusalem on what we commemorate as Palm Sunday. Palms are strewn along his path, along with an ongoing chorus of "Hosanna." The crowd's adulation was in anticipation of a dramatic change that Jesus would bring about. Unlike other would-be messiahs, who receive their fifteen minutes of fame and then disappear into the chaos of the capital city, Jesus makes a beeline to the temple and turns over the tables of the money changers. His act alerts the Roman and Jewish authorities, who then arrest him—and kindles the anger and hostility of the crowd that had recently welcomed him to the city. "Crucify him!" they shout over and over again. Their ecstatic welcome, issued with the expectation that he would throw the corrupt leaders out and take the throne, turned to hate when Jesus failed to deliver.

It is important to distinguish hate from wrath, which comes not from the ego but emerges from the soul. A wrathful response can be quite fierce and emotional. What distinguishes wrath from hate is that wrath is a response to an unjust policy or position, a creed or an action. Hate is personal; wrath is directed at an issue. Righteous anger, which to my mind is a manifestation of wrath, is not about vengeance; rather, it is an intense desire and commitment to rectify a wrong. Turning over the tables at the temple was an act of wrath. Jesus's condemnation was not personal but was directed at the wanton corruption: "My house shall be called a house of prayer; but you are making it a den of robbers" (Matthew 21:13).

The boundary between righteous wrath and venomous hate can be confusing and is often exploited. There are plenty of people who claim to carry the banner of righteousness on a particular issue, but their commitment and actions are fueled by a venom that is personal: they don't so much want to achieve their goal as much as they want to vanquish the other side.

Greta Thunberg is a teenage environmental activist, who has been going all over the world talking about the current and impending ecological disasters due to human-driven climate change. She is passionate and committed. Her continuing witness has generated a large audience and much appreciation—and a lot of resistance, much of it bordering on hate. There are many who are unable or unwilling to see or hear her, because they focus only on certain attributes: they think she is too small (4'11"), or too young (born in 2003), or too privileged (she comes from an economically comfortable Swedish family), or too compromised (she has acknowledged that she is on the autism spectrum with an accompanying diagnosis of obsessive compulsive disorder), or too strident (many of her detractors have dismissed her by saying that she has an anger management problem). Despite all the derision, if not hate, she receives, she remains focused on what she sees, on the big picture. In an address to the United Nations on September 23, 2019, she said: "People are suffering. People are dying. Entire ecosystems are collapsing. We are in the beginning of a mass extinction, and all you can talk about is money and fairy tales of eternal economic growth. How dare you!" Her voice is often filled with wrath over the injustice humankind has done to our planet. And many respond to her wrath with hate, which is almost always the case when a prophet speaks eloquently and consistently to expose the inequities of the world. She refuses to have her message redirected.

I have never met anyone who has overcome or escaped the impulse to hate. People often proclaim that they hate the sin and not the sinner. I am dubious, because in my experience the hatred of the sin invariably seeps into a hate for the perceived sinner. Hate feeds on hate.

My verbal and venal outbursts when I am cut off driving in traffic are expressions of hate. Often, they surprise me. I tell myself that I shouldn't have these feelings or express them in such a hostile way (always with the windows rolled up), but there they are. I would often confess my verbal transgressions (and the hate that accompanied them) during Sunday parish visitations. People were invariably charitable in response, because every person in the room had committed a variation of the same offense. Except for one woman who, with considerable humility, said that whenever she gets cut off on the road, she responds with, "Go in peace to love and serve the Lord." I was skeptical of her witness and asked her what sort of tone she used when she said it. Again, with humility, she said it as though she meant it. I believed her, and for the many years since I have tried to follow her example and bless people whose driving infractions threaten both my safety and dignity. My percentage of success is not much better than a decent batting average: about thirty percent of the time.

I have met other people who manage to make their moments of hate fleeting and feeble because they have learned not only how to be with the hate that erupts from their egos but also how to channel it. In all cases they have a clear understanding of the distinction between hate and wrath, often accompanied by a disciplined spiritual practice that offers up to God their impulse to seek revenge or impart violence. It takes practice, time, and a commitment to the belief that the impulse toward hatred can be contained and minimized.

Desmond Tutu was perhaps best known for confronting apartheid, which for decades was official policy in South Africa. I remember him pronouncing the word in a lecture he gave shortly after he won the Nobel Peace Prize in 1984. "Apart-hate," he exclaimed. The intention of apartheid, he said, is to keep people apart because of hate. He was passionate, courageous, and disciplined: he began every day in prayerful silence and the celebration of the Eucharist. Through his spiritual practice he learned how the hatred that hovered over that land like a toxic cloud affected his ego and his soul. He acknowledged the anger and hatred, but he did not wield it. He was passionate and fierce in his commitment to justice. He fought the evil regime of apartheid, but he honored the innate dignity of his adversaries.

During the period when Bishop Tutu was leading the Truth and Reconciliation Commission in South Africa after apartheid had been dismantled, he was preaching at a public event about the importance of reconciliation. A disturbance broke out in the large crowd. "He was with them!" someone shouted, accusing an attendee of being complicit or actively engaged in torture during the reign of apartheid. Hatred in the form of revenge and anger erupted in a flash, and people began to attack the accused. He was kicked, punched, and knocked to the ground. Bishop Tutu saw all of this and paused in his sermon. He climbed down from the platform, marched over to the violence, pulled the attackers off the victim, and told them to stop. He saved the man's life. The archbishop proceeded back to the platform, his vestments now bloodstained, and continued to preach about God's fierce love and God's insistence that the main work of the Christian faith is reconciliation and justice.

For some terrifying moments, hate found a home in the crowd, mirroring the government-sanctioned hate that had been violently administered for decades, mostly behind closed doors. Bishop Tutu's response was not to deny the hate or shout it away, but to walk into the middle of it and offer a courageous commitment to reconciliation. His were words and actions from the soul, not the ego.

I must confess that I don't have that level of courage. Most of us don't. When faced with hate, most of us want to put up a sign that says, "Go away." Hate is frightening and debilitating and a catalyst for our own visceral impulses to respond in kind.

Hate cannot be banished, nor can it be quarantined. It needs to be named and understood and, when the dynamics are right—which means that our level of courage is high and resources of support are strong—to be confronted. Hate needs to be seen. Not seeing hate—and how it works—generates a form of blindness. So we need to be in relationship—carefully and cautiously—with the hate. All with the hope—which may at times seem misguided, if not myopic—that it can be converted. Hate should never be the last word.

5

THE LANGUAGE OF SEEING

A s a professional purveyor of words over forty years as a preacher, I have developed a reverence for language as it describes feelings, conveys information, and communicates ideas. The way we use language can open up the world; conversely, it can restrict the imagination, close the mind, or put people down. There is power in language, and that power needs to be used wisely and with care, which requires an ongoing awareness of language's meaning—and demeaning.

We normally think of language as a process that primarily involves speaking and hearing, writing and reading. But in my experience, how we employ language has a profound impact on how and what we see. Language can open up one's horizons, and at the same time, language can limit those horizons, or blur them to a degree that they cannot be seen. And if the tone and text of language is particularly aggressive, a message is sent that one should not look at a particular area at all.

There is also what I would call a shadow side to language. Some commonly accepted terms often have the unintended effect of expressing distance from, if not dominance over, certain people and groups. A shadow makes it more difficult for us to see. I first became aware of this dynamic when I was in high school. The civil rights movement was at full throttle, and one of the challenges from the Black community to the white community was to adjust its language when identifying Black people. At that time in my all-white community, we referred to Black people as "Negroes" with a bit of self-righteousness in doing so, considering it to be a step forward from earlier terms. In the demand for full equality, the argument went, language had to be equal. If white people were identified by their color, Black people needed to be accorded the same privilege. And as I began to make the change in language, I recognized that my thinking changed: the language suggested equality, bending my thinking and opening up a reality I was now able to see.

In the course of my lifetime, there have been considerable linguistic shifts in the language identifying Black people. There are many who would argue that the change in terms over the last fifty years is an ongoing dance of meaningless political correctness. My experience is that the changing terms reflect a desire to be with one another, to see one another more clearly, and the language we use serves to foster that dynamic. In addition to being descriptive, language provides structure. And carefully designed structure creates more opportunities for the emergence of the beloved community. It is hard to get it right, so the language needs to keep changing.

What is interesting to note in the linguistic evolution describing people of color is, the language referring to white people has remained constant. White people have always been referred to as white people. There have been some attempts to adjust the terms—"European American" had some traction for a while, but it didn't stick. The consistent use of the term "white" in any and all conversations about race in America suggests a deep-seated cultural expectation that people of color need to adjust in order to be with white people, rather than the other way around. All of which maintains white dominance and inhibits opportunities for seeing clearly the humanity of the Other.

The language we use around race has a direct and powerful impact on how we see one another. There are many other areas in which language has a similar effect. I have identified three—poverty (as previously discussed), guns, and war, in which the language we use can either help us see more clearly or cast a shadow over what we are attempting to express.

Guns

Like most people concerned about the proliferation of guns, I have learned about the growth in deaths from guns, and how states with less-restrictive gun laws experience more gun deaths, particularly deaths by gun suicide.

And I have learned about the uses of language. Early on in my commitment to reduce gun violence (as co-founder of Bishops United Against Gun Violence), I talked about "gun control" at an activists' meeting. The term was generally accepted in the media and elsewhere, but I was immediately admonished by a friend who had been working in the gun violence prevention movement for nearly thirty years. He got started when his brother, an FBI agent, was shot and killed in 1994 when an armed intruder fired his TEC-9 assault weapon at four agents in an FBI office in Washington, DC, killing three agents and wounding the fourth.

For my friend, reducing the scourge of gun violence was personal. "Don't use that term," he firmly told me. "It immediately shuts down conversation between gun rights people and gun violence prevention folk. It just makes things worse. Use 'gun safety.'" He said "gun safety" had a better chance of being heard by the other side, and thus had the potential, however slim, to open up the possibility for dialogue between opposing views. "Gun safety" allowed conversation partners to see the other as sharing a common value; "gun control" tended to reinforce the image of division.

As I began to use the term "gun safety" in my conversations and writing, I became more aware of how deep the term "gun control" is embedded in American culture—and in the media that expresses that culture—and how divisive the term can be. It both feeds the self-righteousness of those who want to limit the use of guns and stokes the resolve of gun rights people to hold on to their guns and claim that the Second Amendment can only be interpreted their way.

Several years later, when I became more engaged in the Gun Violence Prevention (GVP) movement, which is a loose confederation of over 200 groups across the country, I was explaining my work to a woman I met at a national conference on suicide. "Please don't use that term," she challenged me when I mentioned gun violence prevention. "It comes across as arrogant. It is filled with disdain." She told me she was a university professor who established a suicide network in her home state after her husband had killed himself with a gun. For her, the issue was personal. She said she had some significant success in reducing gun suicide in her home state, primarily because they were able to build a coalition of gun rights people and gun violence prevention people to work on solutions. Language mattered, she said; the care they took in using terms to describe their work had a direct effect on how effective they could be. Language was a critical factor in determining how well they could be with one another—how well they were attuned to seeing the cares and concerns of another individual. Careless language or language considered to be condescending, from either side, had the effect of positioning those sides to square off. "What term should we use?" I asked her. She said that "firearm deaths" was a term that seemed to work, at least for the moment. She was open to a better designation, but only if it could serve as a bridge to bring people together.

As long as the culture has been caught up, if not captured, by the term "gun control," it has been focused on interpretations of the Second Amendment even longer. As Jill Lepore points out in her 2018 book, *These Truths: A History of the United States,* our current debate on the interpretation and importance of the Second Amendment—"a well-regulated Militia, being necessary to the security of a free State, the right of the people to keep and bear Arms, shall not be infringed"—has its origins in the 1960s. Shortly before his assassination in 1965, Malcolm X said that "Article number two of the constitutional amendments provides you and me the right to own a rifle or a shotgun." This sentiment was picked up by the Black Panther Party, founded in 1966 by Bobby Seale and Huey Newton, who said that the Black community needed to exercise their Second Amendment rights because it was the only way they could secure their safety and their destiny.

The National Rifle Association took notice, and in short order shifted its mission from "Firearms Safety Education, Marksmanship Training, Shooting for Recreation"—the organizational motto that appeared over the entrance of its headquarters built in 1957—to becoming the champion of the Second Amendment. It was a significant, if not sudden, attitudinal shift. The NRA supported the 1968 gun control bill, which was enacted by Congress after the assassinations of Martin Luther King Jr. and Robert Kennedy. But with the continuing agitation from the Black Panther Party, the NRA responded to—and reinforced—a white backlash and a commitment to the Second Amendment that has only intensified over the past fifty years. For the NRA and its supporters, the Second Amendment has become a sacred icon of freedom. Embedded in that icon is a subliminal conviction that the white-dominant culture needs to be protected from intrusions and threats from people of color. This subliminal message creates barriers that limit the ability to fully "see" others in their shared humanity. Thus the owning and use of guns has evolved from guns serving as tools for hunting, recreation, and sport to guns being the way to preserve white hegemony.

The linguistic challenge is to shift the terminology. The term "gun control" not only polarizes, but over the years it has been used to drive conversation directly back to the Second Amendment. "Gun safety" shifts the dynamic from the Second Amendment to an issue of public health. Over thirty thousand gun deaths a year in America is a public health issue. That over half of those gun deaths are gun suicides (a percentage that continues to climb) is a public health crisis. That four and a half million children in the United States live in households with unsecured weapons is a public health challenge. That households with guns have a suicide rate that is three times higher than households without guns is a public health alarm bell.

"Gun safety" has the potential to build a bridge. A Second Amendment conversation inevitably polarizes. A public health conversation creates space for people to work together. To say that shifting terminology is yet another example of political correctness reduces the power—and importance—of language. We must choose our words carefully.

War

Since becoming an anti-war activist during my freshman year in college, I have seen myself as a "justice warrior." I have easily embraced the justice dimension of the metaphor, struggling a bit with the warrior reference. My reservations about being a warrior have been tempered some by several biblical references, which either acknowledge the inevitability of war ("a time for war, and a time for peace," Ecclesiastes 3:8) or infer that we should prepare to be warriors ("Put on the whole armor of God, so that you may be able to stand against the wiles of the devil," Ephesians 6:11). I felt empowered by being a justice warrior, buoyed by scriptural warrants. And yet over the years I have been discovering, especially in our current polarized climate, that war and warrior metaphors have become more widely invoked with the intended (or unintended) consequence of being divisive, if not oppressive and dangerous. Different language needs to be found if we are to see the issues and one another clearly.

"War is hell" is a simple and profound statement originally attributed to General William Tecumseh Sherman during the Civil War. It has been invoked countless times since. I remember first seeing that phrase, superimposed over images of the horror of war, on the cover of a book or magazine when I was about thirteen. I believed it. War must be hell, because of the violence, death, and the demonizing of the enemy. The pictures and stories proved it.

For most of us, war generates images and memories of national conflict, invariably involving the military. Death is expected, and it happens. Violence is expected, and it can be unrelenting. But in my lifetime, the war metaphor has been applied to situations that have moved beyond fields of battle to various polarizing issues. We have had the war on poverty, the war on drugs, the war on crime—and in recent times we have had the war on COVID-19.

War divides people between allies and enemies. In military warfare, the goal is for the allies to vanquish the enemy, either by their capture or death. In issues warfare, the intent is to vanquish poverty, drugs, crime, or COVID. The war metaphor implies that these threats to the social fabric are the enemy and therefore need to be destroyed. The problem with the war metaphor is that there are whole cohorts of people associated with poverty, drugs, crime, and COVID, and we risk seeing them as collateral damage or, because they are close to the issue, as the enemy. All the while, those who are waging the war on these issues become warriors— empowered with weapons of arrogance and, perhaps even more insidiously, with self-righteousness.

When George Floyd died from asphyxiation after a police officer held his knee on Mr. Floyd's neck for over eight minutes, the arrest, captured on video, generated immediate responses to the apparent brutality, with demonstrations, marches, and protests all over the country, indeed all over the world. The scene tore the veil off the unjust and often brutal treatment that Black people have long received from the hands, weapons, and knees of mostly white police officers.

"Defund the police" became a popular slogan in response to police violence, as if the withholding of funding will have the intended result of changing the culture of policing in the United States. The role of police as warriors goes back further, and the culture of police as warriors is deeper than the funds allocated to them. From the beginning of police forces in America, historian Jill Lepore points out in her article "The Invention of the Police," they have been regarded as being on the front lines in a war. Widely identified as the founder of American policing, August Vollmer, the newly installed chief of police in Berkeley, California, said in 1909, "After all, we're conducting a war, a war against the enemies of society." And who were these "enemies of society"? Thugs, bootleggers, prostitutes, mobsters, and Black people.

In 1965, President Lyndon Johnson declared a war on crime. The war pitted the police against the criminals who threatened the safety of the *polis*, a Greek word signifying a body of citizens. This war has precipitated a weapons race. Though the proportion of gun-owning households has remained fairly steady over the past three decades—most estimates indicate that one-third of American households have guns—the number of guns in these households has increased, with an average of four guns per owner. Of further concern are the illegal guns and "ghost guns," which can be bought over the internet with no identifying registration to the gun itself. The early months of the COVID pandemic saw an explosion in gun purchases: records indicate that two million weapons were purchased in March 2020 alone, double the one million guns purchased in March 2019. Police departments have responded to this surge in guns by adding to their own arms supply. Lepore reports that $8 billion of military weaponry has been sold to police departments since 1997. We have inexorably moved from a war on crime to a weaponized society.

Some say, with deep conviction and passion, that the war on crime is one that must be won—at whatever cost. If left unabated, a war on crime would very likely create a scenario in which more categories of people would be deemed expendable, more lives would be lost, and more guns would be sold. That is a chilling prospect. I would like to think most people desire some sort of armistice, which would generate a less hostile and more open relationship between those who are wary of the police and those who are largely supportive of the police. One way to do that is to discard the jingoistic language and the deep-seated historic dynamics that undergird it.

Community policing, which became a popular initiative in the 1990s, sought to bring police and *polis* together. Police walked the streets, developed relationships, and got to know the community. Trust developed as police officers and members of communities learned to be with each other. Crime went down. Police became citizens instead of warriors. Yet community policing represents a culture change—and not surprisingly it has generated resistance both within some police departments and among those in the populace who see themselves as the champions of law and order. Evidence of a commitment to retain the war/warrior language makes dialogue across difference more difficult, requiring "the other" to also be "the enemy."

And then there are the justice warriors, who, perhaps unintentionally, reinforce the same war/warrior dynamic. Having once identified myself as a justice warrior, I know that there is a pride, if not an arrogance, not to mention a rush of adrenaline, in claiming oneself as a member of a kind of Special Forces unit, an elite cohort with special insight and weaponized information that seeks to right the wrongs of the culture and to level the playing field. The goals may be noble, but the tactics for achieving those goals end up reinforcing the war mentality, running the risk of maintaining a vicious battle between the required two sides. Nobody wins.

If we can train ourselves to see police and *polis* as fellow citizens rather than as warriors, and learn to use that language, we have the possibility of generating greater harmony, because we are working together for the common good, for the benefit of the commonwealth. We are *being with*, *seeing with* greater clarity. Language makes a difference.

Doubt and Cancel

"Unless I see the mark of the nails in his hands, and put my finger in the mark of the nails and my hand in his side, I will not believe" (John 20:25). So stated Thomas when his fellow disciples reported that they had seen the risen Lord in the upper room, at a gathering where Thomas was inexplicably absent. Thomas wanted more than hearsay. He doubted what he was told. A week later Jesus appears again to the disciples. This time Thomas is among them. After offering his peace to the group, Jesus tells Thomas to put his finger and hand in his wounds. Thomas does as he is told and is instantly transformed from a skeptic to an advocate.

Jesus invites Thomas to put his fingers and hands into the place of pain. We aren't told how willing or hesitant Thomas may have been to accept such an intimate invitation, but we can imagine that Thomas did not want to have his heart wounded or broken again. That had already happened when Jesus was crucified.

As our culture becomes even more reactive and polarized, there is a growing reluctance to put our psyches in places of pain. We don't want our hearts wounded or broken. In recent years we have added "cancel culture" to our growing lexicon, which on the surface is an erasure of people whose opinions and positions, particularly of a political sort, are at acute odds with our own. We cancel them because we are outraged at what they think and believe. But the outrage is a form of pain, and we want some emotional distance from it. If we "cancel" them, removing them from what is within our line of sight, we expect to avoid the pain. In my experience, it just makes the situation worse because the pain festers like an old wound.

To my mind, cancel culture has some striking parallels with the proliferation of HATE HAS NO HOME HERE signs. Canceling a person or a group—dismissing them as being unworthy of attention—reinforces the closed environment in which one lives. The intention is not only that an argument cannot be heard, but that the visage of the one making the case should not be seen. The term "cancel" has some resonance with the term "anathema," employed by the medieval Roman Catholic Church to excommunicate or condemn to perdition those who strayed from sanctioned belief or practice. The term "cancel" may have a half-life, but the impulse to separate ourselves from those whose views are different from our own lives on. While humans have behaved like this for millennia, perhaps this new language allows us to see how cruel we can be to one another.

In Matthew's gospel, Jesus instructs his followers how to deal with situations in the community when one person sins against another. Start with one-on-one conversations, he tells them—with an emphasis on listening—to resolve the issue. If that doesn't work, bring the issue to the Church. Then if the offending sinner refuses to listen even to the Church, Jesus says, "let such a one be to you as a Gentile or a tax collector" (Matthew 18:17), people whom Jesus had earlier demonstrated that he wanted to bring into the community, but whom the prevailing religious practice had kept out. Jesus isn't kicking the sinner out but is telling the offended party to move on.

And in Luke 10, when Jesus appoints seventy followers to serve as his advance team, he outlines how they should proceed: "carry no purse, no bag, no sandals; and greet no one on the road" (Luke 10:4). Whenever they enter a house in a community, they are instructed to first say, "Peace to this house."

They are to bring the Lord's greeting and hospitality. If the greeting and hospitality is not returned, "go out into its streets and say, 'even the dust of your town that clings to our feet, we wipe off in protest against you'. . . I tell you, on that day it will be more tolerable for Sodom than for that town" (Luke 10:11–12).

That sounds like a cancel. For Jesus, withholding hospitality is a sacrilege. He won't tolerate it. Withholding hospitality with impunity is not an option. There are consequences. To participate in the human family, one needs to be open to receiving another with a welcome and openness. That is foundational to living together in the human family. It does not mean that people need to agree, or submit, but Jesus insists on the willingness to receive one another as brothers and sisters, and to acknowledge our common humanity. He gives people multiple chances to offer the basic hospitality of honoring one another—of being willing to see one another; but if it is ultimately refused, Jesus is not suggesting they be removed, but rather that they not be allowed to participate—unless and until hospitality is embraced.

Woke

In 2009 journalist Bill Bishop wrote a compelling book, *The Big Sort: Why the Clustering of Like-Minded America Is Tearing Us Apart.* He makes the case that over the past several decades people have been living, working, worshipping, recreating, and vacationing in places where other people are more and more likely to think and vote the same way. Bishop demonstrates that the gulf between different perspectives is growing wider—and people are less willing to understand one another, making it easier to cancel the other side out. If there is no relationship, there is little pain.

On the flip side of cancel culture is the pride in being "woke," yet another relatively new cultural locution. It refers to being awakened to the realities and injustices suffered by others. I am more familiar with woke from the progressive side, but it also exists on the conservative end. Conservatives by and large acknowledge the scourge of slavery and racism, but have become woke to what they portray as an insidious attempt by progressives to rewrite America's past by force-feeding what they consider a skewed history called critical race theory to its students.

Woke progressive people make the claim that they can see systemic racism, white privilege, and the urgency of climate change while others can't or won't. Addressing systemic racism, white privilege, and climate change are laudable and necessary enterprises, but embedded in the language of "woke" is an arrogant belief that some are awake and others are asleep. Implicit in woke language is that non-woke people need to think, speak, *and see* as the woke do. Listening loses out to sermonizing; and any discussion is framed in a calculus of win/lose.

When I arrived in Japan fresh out of college in 1973, I carried some pride with me that I had purged myself of "Ugly American" tendencies, which was the pejorative phrase of the day. My engagement in the anti-war movement had, I thought, cleansed me of cultural imperialism. It hadn't.

About a year into my two-year tenure, something felt off. My Japanese housemates and I weren't understanding one another as well as we had when I arrived. I was missing something. I sought out a graduating senior, who had been the most critical of my presence, for some feedback. He did not hesitate to provide it. He said that I seemed to be unaware (unwoke?) to the fact that I was younger than all the seniors but commanded a level of authority that I didn't deserve (age is a very important benchmark in Japanese culture). He said that all the Japanese students in the house where we lived were committed to speaking in English. Most of them were fluent in the language, but my facility in my native tongue meant that I would invariably win every argument and dominate every conversation. And I was bigger than everyone else, he said, and I lorded my size over them.

I got woke. It was devastating. It broke my heart. But the conversation opened me up to new and uncomfortable dimensions of myself. And because it was so painful, there was a part of me that never wanted to go through that again. I didn't want to be woke again. Which is the problem with woke; it gives the illusion that one has arrived; that one's vision is completely clear. That all the necessary growth has taken place.

Growth in awareness will inevitably involve pain—the pain of our myopia and self-centeredness, and the pain of inflicting pain on others to maintain our own sense of stability.

A corrective to the arrogance of "cancel" and "woke" comes from South Africa and the Zulu (Bantu) language: *ubuntu*. As it has been presented to me, *ubuntu* means "I am because you are." It is deeply relational. *Ubuntu* implies a desire to really see someone else—not as a category or projection, but as another fully actualized human being. It is not possible in the framework of *ubuntu* to cancel each other out because we are linked together, whether we want to be or not. The irony of *ubuntu* is that it comes from a part of the world where cancel culture was official policy, carried out in horrific ways.

To my knowledge there isn't an English equivalent to *ubuntu*. But if there is not a language correlate, there is a process one: listening with respect. Listening not to fashion the most effective retort, which is an ego response; but to listen to and for the soul. A listening that can open our eyes to new ways of seeing. Where is the person's center? How might we be alike? Where and how do we share our humanity? How can we truly see one another? Such a process makes it much harder to cancel, dismiss, or demonize the other.

PART III

Paralysis of Polarity

MANDORLA

"**A**re you Catholic?" the patient asked me, the hospital chaplain.

"No," I told him.

"Then you must be Baptist," he replied. He went on to describe the religious world as he knew it then, some forty-five years ago. As far as he was concerned, you were either Catholic or Baptist. That was it. His was a binary world; most everything boiled down to two choices.

In the decades since, the world has revealed itself to be ever more complex, and societies have become much more diverse. Yet there has been growing pressure to reduce life's issues to binary choices: Catholic or Baptist, Republican or Democrat, Christian or non-Christian, in or out. Polarization is the result, which has been episodic throughout American history, but reached a crescendo with the election of Donald Trump as president in 2016. To an alarming degree people have reduced their choices to Republican red or Democrat blue. Through one form of media or another, vicious verbal salvos are being fired from one side to the other, with the intent of scoring points on, if not dominating or overcoming, the other side. It is nearly impossible not to get caught up in the daily fusillade. Trust gets lost, civility is absent, and a zero-sum calculus appears to rule. The tactics and language are markedly different, depending on whether one is red or blue, but the hardening of positions and the visceral desire to see the other side lose is the same. Seeing differently? Not a chance. More choices? Forget about it.

An earlier president warned of the dangers of factionalism, which tended to reduce issues to binary choices. In Federalist Paper No. 10, founding father James Madison wrote in 1787 (before he became America's fourth president) that there is no "cure for the mischiefs of faction." For Madison, the great fear of factions is that they create an environment in which people care more about defeating the other side than they do about the common good.

In our current polarized climate, there is a temptation to use scripture to reinforce the rigid binary approach to life. In the story of the Last Judgment (Matthew 25:31–46), Jesus prophesies that when the Son of man "comes in his glory" he will separate people as a shepherd separates sheep from goats. The sheep will be at his right hand—and will be welcomed into eternal life; but the goats will be thrown into eternal punishment. The final judgment will be rendered by how we treat the "least of these who are members of my family."

There is clear incentive to be a sheep—to get on the right side and earn eternal life. With that incentive there is pressure to serve others— perhaps with the intent of offering compassion and succor to those who need it but also with a desire to save ourselves: because we will be condemned if we don't serve. There is also a profound temptation, augmented by the virus of polarization, to play the role of the shepherd and condemn the goats in our midst. I/we are in; you/they are out. Binary rules.

What is key in this dramatic biblical story is that before we serve one another, we need to see one another: "when was it that we saw you hungry and gave you food, or thirsty and gave you something to drink . . . and when was it that we saw you a stranger and welcomed you, or naked and gave you clothing . . . and when was it that we saw you sick or in prison and visited you?"

The sheep were able to look beyond their circle and silo—and see the least of these, not as subjects or objects, but as siblings in the human family. Their viewing of one another was grounded in compassion. Their service began with their sight—beyond what they were culturally trained to see. Beyond their socially reinforced, restrictive, and ultimately toxic binary view of the world.

When I first visited Jerusalem in 2005, our small group was taken up to the Temple Mount. It is a strange, if not binary, juxtaposition. Below the Mount is the Wailing Wall, arguably the holiest site in Judaism. Just above is the Dome of the Rock (where it is believed that the prophet Muhammad was taken up to heaven) and Al Aqsa Mosque, known as the third holiest site in Islam. It was a Thursday morning when our guide took us around the mosque, and there were few people milling about. Things would be different the next day, Friday, he said, when the cavernous mosque would be filled with the Muslim faithful for the weekly *Jumma* service. I asked the guide if I could come back. He graciously and clearly said no. "Why not?" I asked. "Because you are not a Muslim," he replied. "How would they know?" I asked again, taking some pride in what people have long said are my Middle Eastern features. He said, again graciously and clearly, that it would take one of the ushers fifteen seconds to determine that I was an American Christian.

"Our survival depends on making these quick judgments. We have been trained."

I was indignant. I thought: Such a prejudicial response. No wonder that region is so frought with conflict. How dare they categorize me so quickly? How shameful that they limit their perspective.

But it didn't take long for me to move beyond my ego-driven dudgeon to realize that I have done the same thing. I was exposed to this sort of sorting out in junior high and mastered it in high school. One's social standing was dependent on how quickly you could determine where someone else fit. Get it wrong and your reputation would be ruined. In my high school we had jocks and nerds, gassers and fuelies, grinds and goofs. It may have taken more than fifteen seconds to figure out what clique people belonged in, but not much more.

My ability to see expanded somewhat in college, during a particularly ugly season of American factionalism, which at the time centered on the Vietnam War. I grew up in a family that trusted the government's messages and believed that our military intervention in Vietnam was both just and right.

During my freshman year, after a college teach-in, at which facts and figures that I had never heard before were presented about the history of US intervention in Vietnam, I was confused. During the milling about after the event I expressed my confusion to a classmate by saying that what we heard was contrary to what we had been told by the government. His response? Maybe the government wasn't telling the truth, a concept that I had never heard or considered before. His response was an invitation to think and see differently, which I began to do. I began to look at information differently, and to seek out other sources for divergent perspectives. I quickly became an anti-war activist. I have long described this moment as a conversion experience, but in retrospect it was an obscure reinforcement of binary choices.

At the end of my sophomore year in 1971, I participated in an anti-war demonstration at Westover Air Force Base in Chicopee, Massachusetts. About five hundred of us were arrested as we staged a sit-in to block the entrance to the base. We were arrested, carted off in buses, and taken to the local police station. The only confinement I experienced was during the ten-minute bus ride to the processing center; any anxiety I might have had was mitigated by the solidarity we felt with one another as we sang anti-war songs the whole way.

When we got to the police station most of us pleaded *nolo contendere*, which was a technical entering of a guilty plea without admitting guilt. I may have had to pay a small fine, but other than that, my illegal activity didn't cost me anything. There were too many of us—and too small a local staff—for them to file a civil or criminal record. I later learned that the costs involved in arresting, transporting, and processing all of us nearly bankrupted the municipality.

I participated in the sit-in because I believed (and believed strongly) that our action, along with innumerable other similar actions across the country, would end the war. I was focused on a goal. I still remember a public lecture given by Willard Wirtz, a former secretary of labor in the Johnson administration who later became an anti-war activist, whose passion reached a fever pitch when he bellowed that our (students') commitment and actions were instrumental in ending an unjust war. His words and conviction had a powerful impact on me and reinforced my resolve. Until US involvement in the war ended in 1974, the anti-war movement framed my life. It focused how I looked at the world and my place in it. It gave me a faction of like-minded people to live with, and an oppressor to protest against. I carried the misguided conviction that the pro-war and anti-war factions were unalterably separate, and that the only way forward was for the anti-war faction to vanquish the pro-war faction. In retrospect, I realize that I merely traded one faction (the government always tells the truth) for another (the government never tells the truth); a trade that precluded me from a deep dialogue with anyone who held different views on the war.

Over the years I have resisted the temptation to reduce issues and concerns to binary options, but the current political/ideological climate renders that more and more difficult. Enter the *mandorla*, an image and concept that was foreign to me until I was introduced to it a few years ago by my spiritual director. *Mandorla* is indeed foreign; it is the Italian word for almond—and refers to the shape that is created when two circles intersect. Many of us learned of this concept, but with a different name, in sixth-grade math when we were introduced to the Venn diagram. It turns out that a significant amount of medieval Christian art is framed in the mandorla, which was intended to depict the intersection between heaven and earth. Images of Mary and the infant Jesus, and of the risen Christ were often depicted within the mandorla.

The mandorla is visually and philosophically distinct from a halo, which is what I have always conjured up in my mind when thinking about Christian religious art. The halo depicted above a character's head, often that of Jesus or Mary, signifies their unique holiness. In contrast, the mandorla represents a *space* that has the capacity to generate holiness and freedom. The mandorla was a new image for me—and it has enabled me to both see and think differently. The mandorla has freed me from the fruitless task of trying to earn my halo by demonstrating how holy or good, or competent or compassionate I am; rather, it serves as an invitation to enter a space where holiness, goodness, competence, and compassion are more possible. The internal pressure to become holy/good/competent/compassionate is hard to let go of; but the image of a space where one might be freed from those internal drivers is, I have found, a space worth aspiring to.

Many scholars think that Hildegard of Bingen (1098–1179), a Benedictine nun, mystic, medical scientist, and visionary, was one of the first artists to depict the mandorla. In her visionary work, the *Scivias* (1151 or 1152), she presented a mandorla of the cosmos. (See next page.)

For me, the mandorla more aptly describes a different way of engaging, particularly in the political polarization that has all but kept our circles apart. As I become more absorbed in the concept of the mandorla, I am less drawn to whatever image might be depicted in its confines and am more entranced by the space itself, the intersection of two circles that can never be fully aligned nor completely separate.

Looking at the mandorla as a metaphor, the more the political tension and polarization escalates, the more people are driven into the core of their circle, with less willingness to acknowledge, much less listen, to the other side. If we see the other circle at all, it is with disdain and mistrust: We end up with a toxic cocktail of projection and vilification, all of which are reinforced by the rhetoric and ideology of those in the same circle. In many quarters the idea of seeing others with curiosity and compassion cannot even be conceived. Verbal violence is permitted, if not

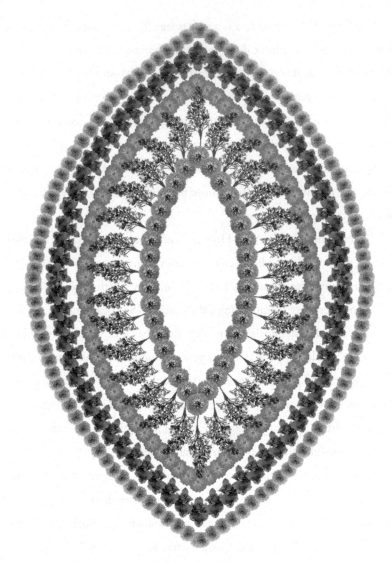

Mandorla, or Vesica Piscis: the image of the almond-shaped halo (radiance) was used as a symbol in medieval Christian art to highlight the figure of Christ. Credit: vavit.

encouraged, and physical violence becomes an acceptable consequence. Nearly every issue demands a binary choice.

While never using the term, Martin Luther King Jr. and Desmond Tutu were leaders who invited, if not challenged, people to enter into a mandorla or a space of reconciliation. In similar ways, each was passionate about making witness to this mandorla space of potential harmony, and each was unrelenting in his commitment to bringing it about. I will talk more about their work and witness in the next chapter, along with Braver Angels, a movement and organization that is devoted to building a bridge between red and blue America. But what the image and concept of mandorla has done for me is to enable me to more fully appreciate what I consider to be the genius of the Anglican movement, in which I am an ordained bishop.

Nearly five hundred years ago the Anglican movement emerged out of the Protestant Reformation. It took several generations, but Anglicanism dared to claim the space between the circles of Roman Catholicism and emerging Protestantism. Between the source of truth being the hierarchy of the church (the Pope, cardinals, and bishops) and the source of truth being scripture (the Protestant priority). The Church of England was the almond between the two religions, one 1,500 years old and the other a fledgling enterprise. Anglicanism could say that it was both Catholic and Protestant; or neither Catholic nor Protestant. It lived—and for the most part still lives—in the tension between scripture and tradition (adding reason as a fundamental ingredient to the mandorla space). From its inception, Anglicanism (and the Episcopal Church) has identified itself as the *via media*, or the way in between.

The in-between space is not a place of compromise, but rather of transformation. The space where heaven meets earth. It is a space of energy—which has the capacity to generate new perspectives, if not new life. It is not an easy space to occupy, for several reasons. For one, the ego seeks stasis, and therefore resists the transforming energy that fills the mandorla space. The ego would rather reside in a silo of safety. Second, it is often emotionally easier to reside in the sanctuary of a familiar circle—and not be challenged by the presence or claims of another circle. Over the centuries Anglicanism has often been more identified with one circle over another, be it the Catholic or the Protestant, the high church or the low church. This was especially true at the outset of Anglicanism, when one faction sought to prevail over the other. Military power was used on both sides. Violence reigned. Lives were lost and reputations were ruined. The chasm seemed too deep and too wide. The Anglican experiment seemed hopeless.

But throughout its history, there remained a commitment to claim the almond, predominantly championed by Queen Elizabeth I (reigned 1558–1603), who sought to build a theological bridge between the two adversarial religious expressions. The almond (mandorla) was nearly erased several times over the next several centuries as one faction within Anglicanism tried to destroy the other—or at least disempower it and reduce it to vassal status. Yet despite all the challenges over the centuries, Elizabeth's wisdom, witness, and legacy lives on. At times the mandorla was squeezed, and many times it appeared to have been crushed—but the transformative power of the mandorla lives on, albeit imperfectly.

In the lead-up to, and the aftermath of, the 2020 election in the United States, political polarization became even more toxic. Millions of people could not even begin to imagine how the circles of Democratic blue and Republican red might intersect, even as the slenderest of slivers. As I talked with religious leaders across the country, I heard more and more people—from both circles—express their disdain for the "other side," and they wouldn't, and in many cases couldn't, see their counterparts as partners in a democracy. Resentment reigned. The idea of a mandorla was relegated to a quaint, if not impotent, medieval image.

Much of the tension gripping the 2020 election boiled down to the conflict between claims of voter fraud and voter suppression. "I can't believe they believe that" became a mantra, uttered from both sides. The legacy of voter suppression in American history, particularly against Black people, rose again from beneath the surface and burst forth. A female colleague of color expressed it best: "How long will we be asked to put our oppression on the altar of reconciliation?"

How long, indeed. Her question identifies the fault line that we are facing and, if truth be told, many want to avoid. The chasm seems too deep and too wide. At moments it all seems hopeless. But there is always a mandorla to be found, because by definition the polarity can never be totally separate, nor can the circles completely overlap. The challenge is to continue to walk into that excruciating tension in the hope—and faith—that something new will emerge.

For an individual to enter into the mandorla space of seeing and being, several commitments are necessary: The courage to confront difference, willingness to listen, and listen deeply to opinions and positions that at first sound disorienting, if not jarring. But most important is the desire to first see someone from another circle or silo not as an adversary but as a child of God who is as deserving of God's full blessing as those who dwell in one's own circle. This desire, which is not always easy to maintain, especially during times of growing polarity, is the necessary first step to reconciliation. Reconciliation doesn't mean that we agree, or that one side has to jettison its beliefs in order to be in relationship with the other side. It simply means that we can dare to be in this space together—with the courage to confront difference, a willingness to listen, and an ongoing commitment to seeing one another as equally blessed.

And, as biologist and writer Merlin Sheldrake writes in his seminal 2020 book, *Entangled Life: How Fungi Make Our Worlds, Change Our Minds and Shape Our Future*, the boundaries between the circles are literally fungible. As much as many would like to claim otherwise, the boundaries are more porous than permanent. In the biological world, fungi find ways to move in and out of ecozones, bringing unexpected nourishment. In the human world of facts, norms, and practices, there are ideas and values that can sneak into silos that would not ordinarily welcome them in, softening edges and fostering listening.

People cannot be forced into the mandorla. There will be moments, if not long stretches of time, when people cannot muster the courage to confront difference, the willingness to listen, and the desire to see someone as equally blessed by God. The anxiety, pain, fear, and hurt may just be too much. That is understandable, and is to be expected. There will also be people, who tend to live at either end of a bell curve, who will refuse any and all invitations into the mandorla. People who won't let go of their need to square off against an opponent—who are unwilling or unable to see someone from the other side as blessed. As long as those extreme beliefs are held, reconciliation is not possible—in the short term or ever.

Throughout his ministry Jesus invited people into a mandorla. He extended his blessing to everyone, even while knowing that some would not accept his blessing or acknowledge that certain people—tax collectors, Gentiles, lepers—were worthy of blessing. When he sends out the seventy to bear the good news, he charges them, as we discussed earlier, to offer God's peace as they enter someone's house, and to announce that the kingdom of God has come near (Luke 10:9). If a welcome is not offered in return, he tells them: "even the dust of your town that clings to our feet, we wipe off in protest against you" (Luke 10:11). In other words, move on. Seek out those who are willing to go beyond a binary choice and risk entering the mandorla.

7

LIVING THE MANDORLA

Martin Luther King Jr.

To my knowledge, the Rev. Dr. Martin Luther King Jr. never referred to the mandorla, but his life and ministry certainly gave witness to it. Dr. King was murdered during my junior year of high school. I certainly felt the tragedy of his death. I admired his faith, his eloquence, and his passion, but I was wary of his overall mission. The all-white community I grew up in admired King from a distance but was largely unwilling to do the work that he called us to do. In that affluent suburb in the Northeast, with layers of racial, educational, and economic insulation, we could say that the problem of racial inequality lay elsewhere, and not with us.

Part of King's genius was his ability both to lead the civil rights movement, with the goal of pushing the politicians and pulling the country into a condition of legal racial equality, and at the same time to invite people into the struggle; into the mandorla. In his famous "Letter from Birmingham Jail," written in August 1963 to a group of "moderate" Birmingham clergymen, all of whom were white, Dr. King passionately and eloquently outlined the history of racial oppression and insisted that his Christian faith required him to speak, write, and demonstrate against it.

Responding to their expressed wish that Dr. King and his followers wait until the rest of the country could catch up to the demands of the civil rights movement, Dr. King said that since "freedom is never voluntarily given by the oppressor, it must be demanded by the oppressed." He indicated that he and his followers had no choice but "to engage in direct action."

His letter is filled with scriptural and historical references, which serve to provide a common language and understanding for his readers, and which are tantamount to an invitation to participation. He then chastises the letter's recipients directly: that moderates are more devoted to order than to justice; that they prefer a "negative peace," the absence of tension, to a positive peace, which includes the presence of justice. Dr. King acknowledges that his words and actions generate tension but suggests that if that tension is not openly acknowledged, it surfaces in oppressive and violent ways. And he indicates that he has no end of examples to verify that. He chastises the church writ large for what he sees as its priority of self-preservation and invites his readers to be the church within the church—the *ekklesia*—where the gospel can more freely thrive. In closing, he expresses a hope that they will have a chance to meet one another, as fellow clergymen and Christian brothers. His is an invitation to white religious leaders to dare to move out of comfort and into the mandorla space, where true freedom has a chance to be born—for all.

His letter reflects his determination to achieve a goal, and his conviction that his strategy of nonviolence baked in love was needed to get there. At the same time, King's letter reflects his willingness to invite the white world to see the oppression and indignity forced on the Black community—and to enter that space of mandorla, so that everyone might be free from the oppression of prejudice, either as wielder or as victim.

In the fifty-plus years since Dr. King's death, and in the wake of scores of murdered unarmed Black men—either at the hands of racist citizens or police—the protective silos of white privilege are slowly breaking down. The systemic racial, educational, and financial insulation of white communities has been exposed, which is a necessary first step. It may be that Dr. King's vision of hope and justice is coming closer to reality. As people of different ages and races took to the streets across the country to protest the killing of George Floyd, I had an image of people willingly and willfully entering a mandorla space, with an insistence that white privilege be exposed and systemic racism come to an end—so that a social, political, and spiritual transformation can take place.

Yet as the demonstrations grew in number, passion, and commitment, there was a predictable resistance to this mandorla opportunity. As has been the case throughout American history, there are voices and forces that want to keep people in their respective spaces so that the white power balance is maintained. The mandorla space is seen to be too risky, because it requires a level of vulnerability to enter. There have been more and more forces of resistance to those peaceful demonstrations and to Black Lives Matter. There have been more forces and voices from the inner reaches of each silo seeking to maintain the binary vision, which precludes the possibility of meeting in the mandorla. To my mind, they are displays of moral emptiness.

And yet. "The arc of the moral universe is long, but it bends toward justice," Rev. Theodore Parker said in a sermon in 1853 that was often paraphrased and quoted by Martin Luther King Jr. The emphasis placed on the tragedies of our racial history feels more intense than at any time I can remember, which could result in a greater bending toward justice.

Braver Angels

For decades the American populace has been riven by polarization, but it was often explained as merely a series of culture wars. With the election of Donald Trump as president in 2016, however, the polarization reached a new crescendo. In 2020, with two deadly viruses—COVID-19 and systemic racism—along with the anxiety in the run-up to the November election, the polarization was acute and threatening.

To an alarming degree, people sought a safe harbor in the comfort of their circle, be it Republican red or Democrat blue. And as the tension continues to grow, there is increasing pressure to retreat to the inner reaches of those circles, where it feels safest. At the center of each circle people tend to see those who reside in the other circle not as competitors but as enemies who need to be defeated.

Almost immediately after the 2016 election, Better Angels was created. The name was taken from Abraham Lincoln's first inaugural address in 1861: "We are not enemies, but friends. We must not be enemies. Though passion may have strained, it must not break our bonds of affection. The mystic chords of memory . . . will yet swell the chorus of the Union, when again touched, as surely they shall be, by the better angels of our nature."

In early 2020, the name of Better Angels was changed to Braver Angels, in part because another nonprofit had already claimed the title, but also in acknowledgment that the level of polarization now made it necessary to draw on the braver angels of our nature.

The intent of Braver Angels is to depolarize America, a lofty and daunting goal. The fundamental component of its work is to gather people in guided conversations, with equal numbers of participants on either side of the political divide, to engage in deep listening. In effect, to find the mandorla. Since the 2016 election, thousands of facilitated conversations have been held. Ground rules of civility and deep listening are honored. Participants engage with one another not to convince or convert, but to foster relationships of mutual respect and, if possible, to find common ground. To see one another as fellow citizens. It is hard work, but work that more and more people across the country want to participate in. There are Braver Angels networks in all fifty states, with coordinators, trained workshop leaders, and lead organizers in each. Out of those conversations dozens of alliances have formed, with participants committed to working together on the agreed-upon goal. They are making a difference in their communities, predominantly because their alliance, forged out of profound political differences, has an integrity and power that can more readily leverage change.

Through Braver Angels a mandorla is emerging between the distinct political circles, with the intent and hope that by being with one another with clear ground rules and trained volunteer facilitators a safe space can be created where transformation and reconciliation can emerge and participants can begin to see one another more fully.

I firmly believe it is the movement dimension of Braver Angels (rather than its organizational dimension) that engages people's passion and commitment. Unlike other movements whose trajectories have a desired endpoint (the anti-war movement, for example, seeking the end of the Vietnam War), Braver Angels is a movement that calls people into the mandorla. The invitation to mandorla living is not a call to water down positions or abandon passions in order to live in the almond, but to find the intersection between very real differences. Some people cannot make the journey to the almond—they take refuge in the certainty of their perspectives, and they can't imagine any sort of overlap, perceiving the possibility as unmerited compromise or outright capitulation. Yet Braver Angels is discovering that there is a deep hunger to seek reconciliation and diminish a polarization that at times feels predatory. Braver Angels is a unique movement—not toward a political center, but to a space of intersection and communication. The more that intersection is claimed, and the larger the almond grows, the greater the chance for transformation, if not revelation, because a new way will open up from this common space. There is risk in this daring movement to be with people who harbor differing political views, but from that claimed common space examples abound for new possibilities, alliances, and respect despite our differences. In this process people can discover the opportunity to be set free from the confinement and blindness of binary choice.

Most movements seek to pull or push people toward a goal, drawing on witness, protest, legislation, and—in some cases—civil disobedience as tactics toward the desired end. An issue is clearly identified and fought against. Significant energy is required for engagement, alongside the commitment to continue and a desire to win.

Whereas other movements may require pulling and pushing, the action involved in Braver Angels is to invite: To invite people into the intersection between their circles—into the almond, the mandorla, where transformation and revelation have an opportunity to emerge. This is not an easy physics to master; those who have been involved in conservative or liberal movements have been trained to see only one perspective. And forced engagement, even in work as helpful as efforts toward mandorla-quality communication, can be counterproductive. The invitation must be natural; the acceptance of it offered willingly.

An act of invitation can seem passive in contrast to our more typical methods of engagement with those who hold views different from our own, but it isn't. A genuine invitation into the almond involves risk and an openness to experience what may happen there, and potentially to be changed by it. It will involve being with people you don't normally want to be with. It will mean seeing and being seen. The movement to engage in invitation requires an awareness of how the ego can become defensive and proprietary, seeking to subvert the whole process, especially under pressure. Desire and discipline are necessary to be able to engage in this space: a desire to be aware of arrogance and the need to dominate, and the discipline to let all that go. It is hard but necessary work.

Desmond Tutu

Archbishop Desmond Tutu had every reason to resist recognition of another approach to faith. In South Africa, a particular Christian interpretation of the Tower of Babel story (Genesis 11:1-9) led to the establishment of apartheid. When God destroyed the Tower of Babel, the result was people being scattered and speaking different languages (babbling to one another). The architects of apartheid determined that this meant God intended for people to be separated, with one group having dominion over another. Most interpretations of the story suggest that God's anger was kindled because people's hubris led them to think they could build a tower to heaven and replace God and rule the earth.

Like millions of others in South Africa, Archbishop Tutu was a victim of the scriptural misinterpretation that justified apartheid. And he fought against it with prayer, which he invited the rest of the world to join. At a sermon he gave at the church I served, in Worcester, Massachusetts, on the occasion of his granddaughter's baptism, Archbishop Tutu began by thanking the throng of people who had packed the church. He thanked us because "Your prayers ended apartheid." He told a story about a nun who lived alone in the woods of Northern California. She wrote to him to tell him that she rose every morning at 2 a.m. and for an hour prayed for apartheid to end. "They didn't stand a chance," the archbishop thundered, "against a solitary nun praying before dawn in Northern California."

There clearly were various political, economic, and cultural dynamics at work that contributed to apartheid's demise, but Archbishop Tutu's witness impressed upon so many of us that our collective vision for justice, blessing, and freedom, expressed in prayer, can move us through competing theologies and beneath the ego's need to dominate, to a mandorla place—where individual salvation and social justice meet, and where we can see the world and our place in it in a new and creative way.

The Anastasis Icon

"*Christos Anesti*" is the Easter acclamation in the Greek Orthodox Church ("Christ is risen"). It is spoken, sung, and depicted in the Anastasis icon (see the next page). At first glance, the icon, also known as the Harrowing of Hell, seems to belie the notion that people can't be pulled into the mandorla. In this famous rendering of the Resurrection, a prominent icon in the Eastern Orthodox tradition, the newly risen

The Anastasis fresco in the Church of the Holy Saviour in Chora, or Kariye Church. Chora Church is a medieval Byzantine Greek Orthodox church. Credit: Zzivet.

Christ is framed in the mandorla, pulling Adam and Eve, who represent all of humanity, out of hell into the almond of resurrection and freedom. What is important to note here is that the two are not being forced into the mandorla: They are beseeching the risen Christ to draw them out of the darkness of hell and into the light of new life. They want to join Jesus in the transformation space, and they have the visible faith that he can bring them there. The implication is that Jesus will remain in the mandorla for as long as it takes to pull people into new life, beginning with Adam and Eve and ending only when the most recent resident of hell desires to be lifted out.

In the Western Christian tradition, images of the resurrection depict the risen Christ, dressed in white and looking very much alive, but he alone has been raised from the dead. If there are Western iconic or artistic renderings of Jesus reaching back to pull others out with him, I have not seen them. My early faith journey was not nurtured by them. The implication of the Western images is that the resurrection is an individual affair. Jesus has shown the way and individuals can accept the gift, get on the road to earning their halos, and join Jesus in new life, one person at a time.

Both the Eastern and Western Christian traditions demonstrate in their theology, worship, and symbols a passionate commitment to and faith in the resurrection. For the first thousand years of the Christian movement, east and west shared the same path. But cultural, historic, and theological differences became too much to hold them together, and their paths diverged in 1054 (when the Eastern Orthodox Church broke off from the Roman Catholic Church). It was a seismic shift within Christianity, and many would argue that Christianity hasn't recovered. Like my hospital patient of forty years ago who divided the religious world between Catholics and Baptists, there is a temptation to reduce Christianity to a binary choice—between individual salvation and communal transformation. Both the Eastern and Western branches of Christianity seek to bring people into the mandorla of new life. There seems to be consensus from the wide array of Christian traditions that new life is the space we want to occupy, but there is hardly a consensus as to what that space looks like, how large it should be, or who can be invited in.

I grew up in the Episcopal church. Our family attended worship every Sunday during the school year. It wasn't so much a reinforcement of a tribal identity as it was a weekly gathering of the herd. We needed to be there to claim our place in the scheme of things. Faith was important, as was worship, but it felt secondary to the affiliation of being in an enclave of other like-minded (and similarly ethnic) people who were committed to being good. As a child I felt that the practice of going to church made me a good person. Not going to church subtracted from my goodness, so I was fearful of not going. The gift of new life would be given to me provided I kept going to church.

By the time I got to college, and a new level of independence, the need to go to church waned a bit and the issue of accepting the resurrection as an integral part of the faith emerged as a choice I needed to make. I had a difficult time making it. As I studied the psychology and history of religion, doubts began to surface. As outlined in scripture, inconsistencies in the Christian story emerged. I was confused, and that confusion was heightened by the conviction of others who had made the individual salvation choice and were rather dogmatic in their expectation that I do the same.

A way out presented itself to me as I became more involved in the anti-war and civil rights movements and the deepening awareness of racial and economic inequity. Social justice was a space I could enter. It offered me transformation and passion, while providing emotional and spiritual distance from the advocates for individual salvation.

How do we begin to understand these differing perspectives? Both the individual salvation beliefs and the social justice starting frameworks are committed to new life—they each discern messages from scripture and from the example of Jesus—but may be reluctant to recognize the presence of the other or acknowledge each other's wisdom. Or accept the idea that we can share the same mandorla, finding those areas of shared faith. We find ourselves too often separated by certainty and arrogance.

And we are back to reducing our faith to binary choices, which ultimately are false choices. Jesus knew this. As the Anastasis icon demonstrates, the risen Christ stands in the mandorla ready to pull us out of the dark theological rabbit holes we have devised and into the transforming space. And the question is, for me and for us, Will we beseech him to do so, or will we remain paralyzed, buried by our egos and arrogance?

— PART IV —

Seeing Our Traditions Differently

8

CREATING MANDORLA
SPACES OF JUSTICE

There is an error in the 1979 Book of Common Prayer. On page 847, in the section called the Outline of the Faith, commonly called the catechism (or teaching), a question is posed: "What response did God require from the chosen people?" In an attempt to quote Micah 6:8, the answer comes back: "God required the chosen people to be faithful; to love justice, to do mercy, and to walk humbly with their God."

Micah didn't say that. Micah said that the Lord required people to do justice, not love it. This is a telling mistake, because it reflects a reality that I have noticed in myself and others over the years: That there is a whole phalanx of people who love justice, who sing and pray for justice, write position papers on justice, but hesitate to do justice. When I was first being trained in community organizing in the mid-1980s, I remember the lead organizer of the Industrial Areas Foundation, which had a long and successful record of working with unions and faith communities, saying that in organizing "you start with conservatives and moderates, and maybe the liberals will come along." As a rather entrenched liberal my-self, I pondered what he meant; and I realized that we liberals can spend an inordinate amount of time trying to get the argument right. To craft the proper stance on a position or policy. There are drafts and re-drafts, and amendments, and amendments to amendments, to the degree that acting on injustice can get lost. All because we love justice.

I wrote my first term paper when I was in the eighth grade: "The Injustices of Our American Society." I faintly remember some of the injustices I exposed in my paper: racism, pay inequity (I couldn't figure why my female teachers earned so much less than the fathers of their students), and wide disparities in the quality of education based on one's zip code. But what I clearly remember is the sense of satisfaction, if not pride, I felt in being a champion of justice. That desire for satisfaction continued through the years—as I conducted charity drives in college and established a soup kitchen and interfaith shelter system early on in my ministry. No doubt these efforts provided needed sustenance and suc-cor for people who needed it, but in some ways the one who was most helped was me. I was doing something virtuous—and it made me feel good. There is nothing wrong with that, but the danger is that it can liter-ally leave one shortsighted.

I felt this as a teenager when I overheard a conversation my par-ents had with dinner guests. The conversation at the table turned to civil rights, and the female guest perked up and said with a level of pride that I couldn't see but could clearly imagine, "Well, I am very liberal on that subject." What I heard in her voice was a self-righteousness that her thinking was out ahead of her conservative friends, which was more important than the issue itself. Her opinions may have translated into some actions, but I didn't think so (which may reflect some arrogance on my part). On a plane several years ago, I heard the passenger in the row behind me telling his seatmate how committed he was to bringing justice to the poor. The guy reeked of self-righteousness. He was loud; I tried to shut him out—and as I did so I realized that the only material difference between his attitude and mine was his volume.

My favorite definition of justice comes from scripture scholar Walter Brueggemann, who has said that justice is sorting out what belongs to whom, and then giving it back to them. In many cases, the sorting out process can be endless, so that the act of giving back may never fully take place. Commitment to justice requires a long view.

Doing justice requires engagement, not just with concepts but with people. It requires moving beyond making arguments on paper and instead putting feet on the ground. It requires building relationships, not just with the people who support the same position, but with those who defend the other side; and particularly with those who are the victims of the injustice. The Western cultural emphasis on consumption subliminally and overtly reiterates that we need more stuff to live a fulfilled life. From these messages, and the other social, political, and economic dynamics in play, a growing gap has developed between those who have more and those who have less. Justice challenges us to work toward a system in which everyone's "enough" is closer together.

Doing justice requires seeing beyond what we want to see. Doing justice requires direct engagement, which means it gets messy, confusing, and frustrating. Doing justice requires getting on an uneven playing field and working to level it out. One cannot adequately do justice from a safe distance.

Martin Luther King Jr. tried to maintain that distance, at least at first. When he received his PhD from Boston University, his first desire was to remain in the north, teach theology at a seminary, and write books. His father, pastor of the well-known Ebenezer Baptist Church in Atlanta, wanted his son to have some experience leading a congregation. His influence prevailed, and Dr. King became pastor of Dexter Avenue Baptist Church in Montgomery, Alabama, in 1954. King's intention was to stay just a few years, but the Montgomery Bus Boycott interrupted his vocational trajectory. As described in *Parting the Waters*, Taylor Branch's account of the civil rights movement from 1954 to 1960, King received an invitation to attend a meeting of the developing bus boycott committee. King agreed to go, to show solidarity with an important community issue. Branch reports that King came into the meeting late—and the ad hoc organizers looked at the relatively new pastor in town and thought: "He's young, he's new, he hasn't made any enemies yet—let's make him the chair of the committee" (he was not the first person to show up late to a meeting to whom that has happened). King agreed, in part to have community involvement as part of his pastoral portfolio. His yes to the offer changed the trajectory of his life—and indeed changed the course of the history of the country. What began as a commitment to serving as a volunteer ended up being a prophetic vocation. As noted earlier, Dr. King liked to quote Unitarian minister and abolitionist Theodore Parker: "The moral arc of the universe is long, but it bends toward justice." For thirteen years, from 1955 until 1968, King committed his life to bending that arc, a commitment that eventually cost him his life.

Doing justice is hard—and depending on the issue and the level of commitment to resolving that issue, the commitment can be fatal—as it was for Martin Luther King Jr., Mahatma Gandhi, and Jesus of Nazareth, whose witness King devotedly tried to follow.

Jesus has a lot to say about justice. To the man who invited him to a banquet, Jesus says, "When you give a dinner or a banquet, do not invite your friends or your brothers or your relatives or rich neighbors, lest they also invite you in return and you be repaid. But when you give a feast, invite the poor, the crippled, the lame, the blind, and you will be blessed, because they cannot repay you. For you will be repaid at the resurrection of the just" (Luke 14:12–14). Bring in those whom society has labeled as outcasts. Bring them in so you can see them—which will then inspire the host to do something about the inequity. If the outcast's situation and its remedy remain only on parchment, actions to correct injustice are not likely to take place. And if the invitees are viewed as tokens and not honored as guests, the entire enterprise is in vain.

Jesus's commitment to justice was rooted in the scriptural tradition. For example, from Isaiah: "Learn to do good; seek justice, correct oppression; bring justice to the fatherless, plead the widow's cause" (Isaiah 1:17).

Seeking justice is hard. It is less dangerous—and much easier—to engage in charity, which to my mind is a form of loving-kindness, and which is on Micah's list of requirements to be faithful. Etymologically, charity connects in Old English to "Christian love of one's fellows." Over the centuries that love has largely been demonstrated, particularly in times of tragedy, through donations of money, materials, and time, donations that are welcome and needed. Americans in general, and Christian Americans in particular, are exemplary in providing charity. Charity is required when people don't have the basics of life—food, shelter, and clothing. In my experience, charity is most immediately offered after incidents of Mother Nature's tragic anomalies—earthquakes, tsunamis, hurricanes, tornadoes, volcanic eruptions. The destruction lasts but a few moments or a few days—but the tragic aftermath can go on for years. And the charity in response can be extraordinarily generous. After the Haiti earthquake in 2010, the diocese I served raised just over $100,000 in three weeks for Episcopal Relief and Development, a trusted agency with years of on-the-ground experience in Haiti. Years later, the lockdowns imposed as a response to the coronavirus generated gracious, generous, and creative offerings of charity—from people paying restaurants, house cleaners, barbers, and babysitters for meals and services that they didn't receive; to wealthy people sending their private jets to other parts of the world to collect much-needed medical equipment; to people bringing food and other necessities to quarantined neighbors.

These and other examples are inspiring demonstrations of compassion, and they are offered to ease the pain, and to return life to "normal," for those who have suffered a tragedy. Back to some level of homeostasis.

Doing justice, however, makes the claim that what is normal is, in fact, not normal. It is seeing beyond what we want to see. The pandemic and subsequent lockdowns tore off the veil on an economic and racial system that is inherently inequitable. People living in economic stability could work from home and retain their income and safety, whereas people in the direct service industry were more exposed to the virus and had to keep showing up to work to get paid (and by and large being paid much less than people who remained at home). There was enormous desire to get back to normal; but underneath it was a desire to put the veil back on, and to limit what we see. The pandemic has brought an opportunity to put our collective hand into the world's pain, as Thomas was invited to do with Jesus. Where we have done so, it has often been with the expectation and desire that we pull our hands back out of that wound as soon as we can. Justice requires keeping the hand in longer.

And it is critical that we put our hands into that pain. I once heard the Nobel Laureate Elie Wiesel tell a story from the Jewish Midrash about how Job came to suffer so intensely. God called in Job and two others for advice as to what God should do about the enslavement of the Jewish people in Egypt. "Let the people go," one of them said. Another recommended that they remain in slavery to burnish their faith. As for Job, he said, "I am neutral; I have no opinion." And for that non-response, the Midrash story continued, Job was punished. Another Nobel laureate, Desmond Tutu, wrote, "If you are neutral in situations of injustice, you have chosen the side of the oppressor." We not only need to see dimensions of the world's pain, we need to put our hands in it.

There is a much-told fable about an ancient village located on a river. One day a villager noticed a baby in a basket floating down the river. He waded in, fished it out, and took care of the baby. The next day two babies in baskets were fished out. And so it went for many days, and in short order the village developed a baby rescue agency, which required the assistance of nearly everyone in the village. After several weeks, the villager who rescued the very first baby broke ranks and said he was leaving and was not going to help with the work of caring for the babies any more. He was told that they needed everyone to take care of the babies—to keep the system going. Where was he going that was so important that it threatened their system? "I am going upriver to see who is sending down the babies," he replied.

Justice requires going upriver, to a different place, and seeing from a different perspective. In his 2011 book, *Toxic Charity*, author

Robert Lupton makes the case that relationships built on need are seldom healthy, nor do they reduce the need itself. The giver–receiver relationship is doomed from the start, because it is not designed to foster much-needed trust. Instead, the giver–receiver relationship can breed resentment and dependency—on both sides. The author of Deuteronomy makes the case for justice:

> You shall not pervert the justice due to the sojourner or to the fatherless, or take a widow's garment in pledge, but you shall remember that you were a slave in Egypt and the Lord your God redeemed you from there; therefore I command you to do this. When you reap your harvest in your field and forget a sheaf in the field, you shall not go back to get it. It shall be for the sojourner, the fatherless, and the widow, that the Lord your God may bless you in all the work of your hands. When you beat your olive trees, you shall not go over them again. It shall be for the sojourner, the fatherless, and the widow. When you gather the grapes of your vineyard, you shall not strip it afterward. It shall be for the sojourner, the fatherless, and the widow. (Deuteronomy 24:17–21)

Provision must be made for the widow, the fatherless, and the sojourner. That is a noble and necessary gesture, yet the provision is for what is leftover after the harvest. That is charity, but not justice. Justice would require that everyone share in the first fruits of the harvest, not its dregs.

Indigenous Australian artist Lilla Watson spoke to this resentment in 1985 at a United Nations Women's Conference: "If you have come here to help me, you are wasting your time. But if you have come because your liberation is bound up with mine, then let us work together." Her comments are well remembered, and indeed identify the challenge to see one another in a mutually liberating way.

In 2018 former *New York Times* columnist and current New York University professor Anand Giridharadas wrote a best-selling book titled *Winners Take All*. He exposes the fallacy of "win-win" situations, in which well-respected, high-priced management consulting companies bring their strategic planning, algorithms, and economic models to bear on intractable problems in the developing world. They have designed winning formulas that they predict will produce big "wins" in areas of poverty, food insecurity, and health problems. The intentions are noble, the theory works in certain places, but the processes are imposed. If relationships develop at all, they are based on the imported model, and not the other way around. Culture tends to be reduced to a metric. The long and the short of it: these interventions don't work. Adequate time and space are not given over to seeing the landscape. The giver–receiver dynamic continues, and resentment builds.

Charity is a biblical value. It can provide wonderful and much-needed help, particularly in times of crisis. But the shadow side of charity is that it doesn't level the playing field, and it can limit one's vision. It can be infused with a desire to have one's own need for satisfaction met. As a result, it can reinforce the inequity that is already there. In a strange but perverse way, the charitable giver benefits from the injustice, because the giver is allowed to remain as the giver, able to keep a distance that mitigates against transformational change. As Giridharadas has written, charity boosts the reputation of the giver, and creates dependency in the receiver.

As there is a tension between charity and justice, so is there a tension, if not a conflict, between the priorities of reconciliation and justice. There are many who make the case that reconciliation can be achieved only after justice is reached. Justice comes first, the argument goes. In the catechism of the Book of Common Prayer, mentioned at the beginning of this chapter, the question is posed: "What is the mission of the Church?" The answer is short and presumably clear: "The mission of the Church is to restore all people to unity with God and each other in Christ." To restore: Is that reconciliation or justice? Or both? Too often reconciliation comes at the expense of justice.

Jesus speaks to this challenge: "So when you are offering your gift at the altar, if you remember that you brother or sister has something against you, leave your gift there before the altar and go; first be *reconciled* to your brother or sister, and then come and offer your gift" (Matthew 5:23–24). Jesus's words (which are the scriptural foundation for the Exchange of the Peace in the eucharistic liturgy) suggest that reconciliation needs to come first.

Like many, I struggle with this tension between reconciliation and justice. I am beginning to see that the conflict over the priority of justice over reconciliation—or vice versa—is yet another invitation into the mandorla. Applying the framework of the mandorla, reconciliation and justice can never be separate, nor can one fully absorb the other. We need to sit in that almond of intersection—and see the urgency of both. In many ways the reconciliation/justice tension is a Christian *koan*, a paradoxical riddle. It is not an either/or proposition, but a both/and—one we need to ponder until something new emerges. We need to be able to see both the need for reconciliation and justice—and develop the ability to discern when and where different orderings of priorities are required.

At the end of apartheid in South Africa, Archbishop Desmond Tutu led the Truth and Reconciliation Commission, which provided an opportunity for the perpetrators of violence in the service of racism to tell their stories and be restored back into the community. While it was the case that the Truth and Reconciliation Commission began its work after Nelson Mandela was freed from prison and elected president and a new constitution was established, each an important benchmark of justice, the desire to have oppressors tell their stories, which is a fundamental component of *ubuntu* (restoring offenders to humanity if they tell their truths), was a driving factor. Reconciliation and justice went together.

In any case, simply loving justice is not enough. Charity often only places band-aids on the world's wounds. Until we make a commitment to *seeing* beyond an immediate crisis and take the time and discipline to look out into a world that continues to support systems of inequity—an ongoing discipline that requires time, space, listening, mutual recognition, and respect—justice and reconciliation will not be served.

REFLECTIONS ON THE COMMANDMENTS

As a boy, I learned the Ten Commandments shortly after I memorized the Lord's Prayer. Maybe it's more accurate to say that I didn't really learn them beyond knowing that there were ten of them, and that I had better obey them. I took some comfort in the fact that when they were presented to me in Sunday school or church, I realized that I pretty much kept them: I didn't steal, I honored my parents, I didn't commit murder, I didn't covet, I didn't lie (or at least much). I wasn't exactly sure what adultery was, but I figured I didn't engage in it. I saw the commandments, particularly the last six, as citadels of proper behavior, and I figured there would be hell to pay if I broke them. So I didn't.

What I didn't understand as that young boy was that the commandments were a short and firm set of guidelines for a group of people who, having escaped slavery, were enjoying their first experience of living in freedom. For generations, they lived under the boot of Pharaoh's oppression, doing his army's bidding, rendered silent by overlords. With their escape into Sinai, they needed to learn how to live together in community, without a despot overseeing their every move and listening to every word.

It was not easy. They were disoriented, hungry, and worried. Several times during their Sinai sojourn, Moses went up a mountain to sort things through with the God who had engineered their escape. God recognized that the people needed some rules to live by. And following one of his descents from a mountain, Moses presented some tablets inscribed with the Ten Commandments: three are about God; six are about how to live with one another in community; and one, the fourth, about the Sabbath, looks forward to the final six and back to the first three. These laws are *apodictic*, meaning they are commands, as opposed to *casuistic* laws, which spell out the consequences if you break a rule. I learned the distinction between the two types of laws while studying the Old Testament in college, but as a youngster all the commandments were casuistic to me: there was always an "or else" appended to each of them. I lived in considerable anxiety over what might happen to me if I got caught breaking one of them.

While I was able to honor most of the commandments, I got stuck on the third: you shall not take the name of the Lord your God in vain. I was taught it meant that I shouldn't use "bad" words. Most people I knew had a version of that lesson drilled into them, with the understanding that if they transgressed that commandment, various forms of punishment would be administered. There was a very long list of words that I wasn't allowed to say; and for many of my early years, my obsessive sense of propriety with the Ten Commandments mandated that there were words I wasn't even allowed to think.

Mandating a list of "unthinkable" words, of course, isn't particularly successful at any age. The words that came unbidden to my childish thoughts scared me, because I carried within me an approximation of the translation of the third commandment, contained in the Book of Common Prayer: "you shall not invoke with malice the Name of the Lord your God." For me, such bad thoughts and the words that gave shape to them were malice. Bad malice. The thoughts were rarely verbalized; that would just make things worse.

The shame of that early understanding stayed with me for a long time, reinforced by my rather narrow understanding of the third commandment, a perception shared by most people I have met over forty years of ministry. For me and my ordained colleagues, when conversation partners discover that we are clergy, their language either cleans up or they apologize for the words they don't think they should have said. Initially I thought their discomfort had to do with a concern that their words might have offended me; over time I began to realize they were assuming that I was not so secretly passing on their transgressions to a divine presence they may or may not have believed in. And whether a believer or not, the threat of punishment after a breach of the third commandment fostered some deep-seated anxiety, if not fear.

These recurring instances have created several levels of dissonance. For one, the sudden pasteurization of language set me up as a language cop, a role that I found profoundly limiting, if not offensive. It also reinforced a common notion that God is a distant deity, who only comes onto the scene when we speak bad words (or engage in bad deeds) and then metes out a consequence from a dizzying menu of punishments, which are dependent on the theology one endorses or the church one attends.

Ultimately, the limiting of the third commandment to an issue of language truncates the whole enterprise. The commandment is not about how we abuse God with our words, but how we use God to advance our own agenda. The focus is not on the Lord's name, but on taking it in vain. In other words, don't say you believe in God if you don't. And don't think that God is some tool you can use when it suits. I had a parishioner once who said with great pride that he kept God in his back pocket, and whenever he needed help, he pulled God out, and let God do what God does, and then put him back in the pocket. What I didn't say in response, but certainly felt, is that such an attitude and belief trivializes God.

As disdainful as I was of this particular parishioner's comments, I have often carried out a version of his practice as well. I haven't kept God in my pocket, but I have often remanded God to some corner of my psyche, to access when the need arises. And then I've stuffed God back into those far recesses when the situation was over. Along with so many others, I have often made the arrogant claim that God is on my side, or our side, which to my mind now is the most egregious breach of the third commandment that anyone can make. The United States is awash with no end of claims that God is on "our" side, which conjures up a world of competing deities. When pundits, politicians, or theologians maintain that God is on their side, the clear implication is that God is not on someone else's side, that God couldn't possibly be aligned with an opposing perspective.

When God becomes an issue of political or theological turf, God is then reduced to a mascot or a back pocket trinket that can be trundled out when needed. Such a perspective demeans, if not damns, God. God is not a means to an end; God is an end. Much as we might like to, we don't own God. Yet there is now no end of political agendas and religious positions that infer, if not outright claim, that God is unequivocally on their side, that God will do their bidding, and not someone else's. God's charge to the human family, as expressed in the third commandment, is that the only side God has ever been on is God's side. Our work is to be with God, not to self-righteously invite God to come and be with us.

When we identify God as being on our side, we set up a delusion that we can see God according to our own design and desire. God then can be taken in and out of our back pocket. When we can claim instead—as the Third Commandment requires—that God is on God's side, and not some fabricated image that advances our agenda, our vision expands and our horizons broaden. And we are then invited to peer into the mystery: to see the unseen.

The disciples never really learned this. "Teacher, we want you to do for us whatever we ask of you" (Mark 10:35), James and John demand of Jesus. When the time comes, they want to have front-row seats in heaven. They may know they are breaking the third commandment, but their intense need for special favors is all they can see. "It is not mine to grant," Jesus responds, "but it is for those for whom it has been prepared" (Mark 35:40). In other words, line up with God; don't ask God to line up with you.

The Fourth Commandment

For me, as a boy, lining up with God meant going to church. That was how to obey the fourth commandment: "Remember the Sabbath day and keep it holy." Going to church was a family ritual that we faithfully followed between September and June—from as early as I can remember, until I went off to college. The church service itself may have provided some moments of Sabbath, but the weekly Sunday morning task of getting four kids up, dressed, fed, and into the car—at the same time, without the dog, which was the only day of the week this logistical challenge was attempted—was all frenzy. There was nothing Sabbath-like about it. But that didn't matter. We went to church. We kept the Sabbath, and if I didn't go, I felt ashamed. Not going to church meant that some punishment was in store: it might not be levied for several decades down the road, but it would come.

Engaging in worship is indeed an important part of the Sabbath. Worship is meant to remind us of who we are and whose we are. Old Testament scholar Walter Brueggemann has often remarked that a primary function of worship is the public processing of pain. When they were enslaved in Egypt the Jews were not allowed to voice their pain, so they groaned privately—a groaning that God eventually heard and offered God's promise of freedom (Exodus 3:8). Since the days of Jewish slavery in Egypt, every totalitarian or despotic state has forbidden public expressions of pain or protest, with terrible consequences if the ban is breached. The oppressed are kept silent. Worship allows for pain to be expressed to a God who hears and offers hope, if not release.

Brueggemann also talks about the difference between the presumed world and the proposed world. In the presumed world people can expect that if they work hard and keep the Ten Commandments, things will work out for them. Dominant classes, which in the West have been white people of European descent, are imbued with the benefits of the presumed world. Worship may offer visions of a proposed world—of hope and equality—but often beneath that offering is a presumption that the people who have lived in privilege will remain there. Which is, for the most part, what people of privilege want to hear and see.

By and large, among oppressed classes, races, and groups, the presumed world is a fiction. Actually, the presumption is that the rights and privileges of the historically favored races, classes, and groups will be preserved at the expense of everyone else. Throughout American history there have been theologies that have argued that it is necessary and good for there to be an identified underclass, in order to preserve the privileged class who then, in their supposed advanced thinking and compassion, will take care of those who live below. In this framework, worship for the privileged can take on the nuance of safe continuity. Pain may be acknowledged, but it need not be felt; nor do those who suffer pain need to be seen.

Since the presumed world has little if any purchase with those who are in the oppressed races, classes, or groups, worship presents visions of the proposed world through prayer, sermons, witness, and music: a world of freedom, equity, and justice. The proposed world is framed in hope, which theologian and activist Jim Wallis describes as "believing in spite of the evidence, and then watching the evidence change."

It takes some time for worshipers to absorb the message and hope of the proposed world. A monk friend of mine, who spent some time in apartheid South Africa, told me that people would often spend up to six hours in church on the Sabbath being filled with the promise of the proposed world, so when they returned to the ignominy of the presumed world, they could cope better, holding on to hope.

The Sabbath is a day of equality. Sabbath is a time/day when we are freed from the consumption/production system. A time/day when we don't need to prove our value and worth to someone else, and most especially to ourselves. A day when we are given the chance to resist the hierarchies that our culture and egos create. An opportunity to see one's self and all others as children blessed by God.

The Ten Commandments in general, and in particular the fourth commandment about the Sabbath, are an attempt to shape power differently.

This is not easy to do, which is exactly the point. The Sabbath is not a time to do, but to be, and that is hard. For one thing, we struggle to find the time to break from doing. In our culture, busyness is regarded as a prime virtue, and since most of us have a vast assortment of electronic devices that pump out messages at a machine-gun pace, we can easily remain busy if we keep them at the ready, which most of us do. At the very least, we remain distracted, which can appear as being busy, both to ourselves and to others.

I have a friend who says that our activities in life can be boiled down to three dimensions: work, worship, and play. She goes on to say that in our current world we tend to worship our work, play at our worship, and work at our play. I think there is some disturbing accuracy in her observation, in that all three of these inversions involve an emphasis on doing, particularly when it comes to worshipping our work. There is little or no time left for simply being, which means there is very little space for Sabbath.

When we are doing, there is a trained tendency to keep score. How much did we get done, how much is left to do, how does our skill or output compare to someone else's? And then there are all the metrics, official or intuitive, or the rankings that we create, external and internal.

Inequality results from these ego-generated impulses. And as we have seen, economic inequality is becoming an ever-widening chasm, partly because there is such an emphasis on doing, getting ahead, and winning, all of which can be a culturally supported exercise in avoiding pain. When we strive to get ahead, we are leaving people behind. And there is the temptation to think that the more we can get ahead, the more likely it is that we can leave pain behind as well. And if the chasm between those who have and those who don't is deep and wide enough, we can subscribe to the illusion that pain cannot make it across the gulf.

Remembering the Sabbath is not going to fix the dangerous divide of economic inequality. But honoring the Sabbath, and honoring the Sabbath regularly, provides the space and time—and the possibility—for us to *see* one another as equally beloved in God's eyes. And if we can see that God blesses us equally, we just might be able to recognize an equality with each other as well. That transformational attitude of learning to embrace human equality will hopefully have an impact on economic inequality, because it entails a recognition of a shared desire to be with one another.

* * *

For a few months during my sophomore year in college I practiced yoga with a small group. We met on wrestling mats in the gym. The group was led by the wrestling coach, who was a bear of a man with a gentle soul. He led us through a very slow cycle of yoga positions, concluding with several minutes of sitting in silence. I responded easily to his leadership, but my mind kept working and wondering as we went through the various yoga poses: Who is winning? How can I get better at this? What is my score? He created Sabbath space, but I couldn't enter it. I was too busy.

On the last day of his earthly life, Jesus struggles in the Garden of Gethsemane. He knows that he is about to be arrested and tortured, and he begs out of the ordeal he is about to go through: "My Father, if it is possible, let this cup pass from me" (Matthew 26:39). Understandably, he wants out of the approaching emotional, spiritual, and physical pain. But in the next phrase, he says, "Yet not what I want, but what you want" (Matthew 26:39). My guess is that there was a time lag between his wanting out and resubmitting himself to God's will. However long it was, it enabled Jesus to claim a Sabbath moment; to let go of the needs of his ego and be reconnected to God.

We need a Sabbath day to remind us that we can be freed from the production/consumption system. We need a Sabbath day to shift our vision from tasks and obligations and into the time and space that allow us to see our world not as something to be managed or even figured out but as a space where joy and freedom can emerge and be celebrated. Where we can have the opportunity to see life as a gift. And we need Sabbath moments to let our minds slow down and allow our souls to emerge. Instead of trying to stifle our well-trained competitive instincts, Sabbath time can enable us to acknowledge their power, which in turn can help to reduce their presence and force. And can give us a deeper appreciation of the power, and need, for the fourth commandment.

The Ten Commandments were non-negotiable, yet humankind has attempted to negotiate them ever since Moses came down from the mountain. Our attempts to domesticate them by focusing on individual purity not only rob the commandments of their ability to reframe how we live with one another but also truncate our imagination to see one another as equals. This broader view of the Ten Commandments frees us from a system in which we *see* God and neighbor as tools of utility, and instead challenges us to see God and neighbor as vital to the developing of a beloved community.

10

WRESTLING WITH FAMILY

M uch of the time we can choose the people we want to be with. Not so with family. Biology chooses our family; we have no choice in the matter. Now it may happen, and often does, that people are cut off or cut out from their family, or circumstances arise so that some members become resolute in their desire not to be with others in the family for a while or for a lifetime.

Despite this, over the centuries the nuclear family has become the primary social unit. We cherish families, and at the same time we are challenged by them. There are times in most of our lives when we desperately yearn to be with family, and there may be other moments when we can't imagine anything worse. We study families, because the dynamics operating within a family, system get played out in society, in our work or professional environments, and in the family of nations. As we learn about families, we learn about culture and about our alternating needs to be with or be apart from one another.

One of the oldest studies on a multigenerational family is contained in the book of Genesis. These files are not confidential; we have been reading and learning from them for thousands of years. What's good and helpful about these files is that they haven't been redacted to the point that the betrayals, resentments, dysfunction, greed, and fear have been airbrushed out.

The case file on this multigenerational family begins with the story of Abraham and Sarah and the birth of their son Isaac and continues down to his great-grandson Joseph (Genesis 17–50). In the middle of the file is the account of the twins; Jacob and Esau, whose story provides valuable perspective on where we are today as a human family—and the struggles we find ourselves in to be with each other.

Jacob and Esau's mother, Rebekah, was infertile for years. When she discovers she is with child, she rejoices in her good fortune, but struggles with the pregnancy. She takes her suffering to her Lord, and her Lord responds: "Two nations are in your womb, and two people born of you shall be divided; the one shall be stronger than the other, the elder shall serve the younger" (Genesis 25:23). Not a very consoling message to a woman who had longed to become a mother, but a prescient prediction.

Rebekah becomes the mother of twins. The first child, Esau, by virtue of birth order, will eventually inherit the family wealth. Holding on to Esau's heel as he is born is Jacob. As the younger son, Jacob will inherit nothing. Esau and Jacob wrestled with each other in the womb, and we can presume they struggled with each other in their youth. Esau was a hunter and was favored by his father. He liked to be outside. Jacob stayed inside the tent with his mother, who favored him. The case file reports that Esau comes back one day from hunting and declares that he is "famished." He points to the corner of the tent and says to his younger brother, "Give me some of that red stuff." Jacob is ready to serve Esau, but only if Esau sells him his birthright. Since Esau can't see life beyond his next meal, he readily agrees. Jacob takes the birthright in return for bread and lentil stew, and after some time goes to his father, Isaac, from whom he needs a blessing. Isaac is now old, disoriented, and blind. Jacob identifies himself as Esau to his father; he puts the skin of a goat on his hands and neck to mimic Esau's hairiness (with Rebekah's encouragement), feeds his father, and asks for his blessing. Thinking that Jacob is Esau, Isaac gives the blessing, and Jacob is now in formal possession of the birthright. A little while later Esau comes into the tent, identifies himself to his father, and he and Isaac immediately recognize that they have been cheated by Jacob and Rebekah. Both are furious, and part of their ire is the realization that the ruse cannot be reversed. The blessing of Jacob as the inheritor is final.

The case file of the sons of Isaac has some intriguing parallels to the story of the American family. Beginning in 1619, white Europeans stole the freedom of Africans, and they were brought to the "new world" as slaves. They were eventually freed nearly 250 years later, but white Americans in its white-dominated culture continue to operate as if they still own a birthright to privilege and authority. In many cases and quarters, the descendants of slaves are not recognized as legitimate members of the American family. And not only did white Europeans steal the freedom of millions of Africans, they stole the land of the people who were already in America when they arrived.

There have been, and continue to be, forces and factions in the United States that want to redact, ignore, or dismantle the American story. To airbrush out the deceit, greed, betrayals, resentments, violence, and fear. To proclaim, without reservation or reflection, that America is the greatest country on earth. Yet to become a robust, open, and community-oriented society, we must understand the complex dynamics of the American family.

We need to see the full story.

After realizing that he has been deceived by his now senior brother, Esau seeks revenge. Rebekah gets wind of his plans and warns Jacob, who flees to Rebekah's brother Laban in a distant country, where Jacob begins a new family. While there, Jacob is cheated by his father-in-law, and in turn Jacob cheats his brothers-in-law. As it turns out, this is a very thick case file.

Decades later, Jacob appears to have a change of heart; he wants to reconcile with his brother (Genesis 32:5). He sends a message to Esau that he wants a family meeting. A response comes back: Esau is willing, and Jacob becomes terrified by the prospect of what he has set up. He presumes that Esau will steal his wealth and kill his family.

Buried in the case file is an account of what happened the night before the brothers' reunion. Jacob is alone; he has sent his family and flocks to the other side of the Jabbok River, where they will be safe. In the middle of the night an individual comes along and begins to wrestle with Jacob. It could be a man or an angel or God. The wrestling match goes on all night, and by dawn it becomes clear that Jacob will prevail, but not before his hip is put out of joint, and he is left with a permanent limp. Before they separate, Jacob asks to be blessed, which the man (or angel or God) obliges. And which enables Jacob to see in an entirely new way. Seeing more clearly requires effort and discernment.

In the morning, Jacob sends out tribute to his brother, flocks of goats and camels and sheep, in an effort to buy Esau's favor. His tactic seems to work until Jacob sees his brother appear with an army of four hundred men. Jacob considers himself done for.

But Jacob swallows his fear and shame and goes out to meet his brother. Instead of taking vengeance, Esau "falls on his brother's neck" (Genesis 33:4) and kisses him. It is a dramatic moment of reconciliation. There are those who might want to claim that the brothers lived happily ever after. It was an enduring reconciliation, but it was fragile. They spent the rest of their lives working on it.

Betrayal, reconciliation, blessing, and an enduring limp. Case closed—but not really.

In many ways the story continues long after the series of encounters near the Jabbok River. The American family has, for generations, been wrestling with the theft of slavery and the racism and prejudice that justified it. Recently, there have been some hopeful signs. In the wake of George Floyd's murder, more stories are being told that enable those of us listening to have our eyes opened to the realities of prejudice and hate. These stories are being told by the receivers of racism and violence, and as more people listen to these stories, the storytellers are getting bolder and more vulnerable in telling them. As the process continues, more and more people are absorbing the pain and injustice and the need for reconciliation, if not reparation. This will need to involve much more than camels, goats, and sheep. Sometimes this wrestling with stories and unseen realities breaches boundaries, which the detractors try and exploit, but for the most part the wrestling is painful, yes, but honest and infused with hope. These are important steps in creating a beloved community.

In 1992, I was rector of an urban church in New Jersey. The country, community, and congregation were feeling considerable tension after the

Rodney King verdict in Los Angeles, which had exonerated the white police officers who had pulled Rodney King out of a car and beaten him senseless. Riots broke out across the country. The "wrestling" was ugly.

In my congregation, we decided to hold a forum in the church to talk through our feelings and concerns. Initially the conversation was careful, if not guarded. It reflected a reluctance to go deeper. The mood changed when one of the wardens of the congregation, a Jamaican dentist and mother of two children, stood up and in tears talked about the fears she had for her then seven-year-old son; how she worried that when he was old enough to drive, he would be pulled out of his car and roughed up, or worse. Her witness was real and raw. People listened—and for many of the white people at the forum the issue of race moved from what they read about in the newspaper or saw on TV, to a story from someone they knew and trusted. They could see in a new way. More people could see that they shared the same birthright.

The Jacob and Esau story demonstrates that reconciliation requires commitment, courage, and time. It can be achieved, but it is often fragile, and needs to be worked at. As America has been learning (for those who wish to do so), reconciliation within the human family is fraught with challenge, especially when we acknowledge the betrayal and misperceptions we have inherited and perpetuated around the issue of race.

Jesus tells a story about the sowing of seeds (Matthew 13:3–9; 18–23). Some seeds fall on rocky ground, some on a path, some among thorns, and some in good soil. Each has different outcomes, from the rocky ground producing no growth to the good soil producing fifty to a hundredfold.

Jesus continues to sow seeds among us, including the seeds of racial justice. Some of those seeds fall on rocky soil—in places where people say racism was once a problem, but is no longer—"Get over it." Some fall on the path, among people who will say, yes, Black lives matter; but upon further reflection say blue lives matter and all lives matter. With so many differing perspectives on the path, the seeds of racial justice get choked out by competing, dominating growth. Some of the seeds fall among thorns—among people who are distracted by COVID-19 and the fragile economy—which are constricting, if not crippling. And then there are the seeds that fall on good soil, among people who are listening and learning, and who are willing to see the challenging work of racial reconciliation, and then do something about it. Abundant growth can happen there.

What I have learned as a gardener is that the soil can indeed produce abundance, but it requires work. I have mulched and added proper soil treatments. I have weeded. And weeded.

The abundance is possible, but it is also fragile. I need to keep weeding. Often, the weeds are interconnected with the good growth (Jesus used that image in his parables, too), so care must be taken as one continues to work at it.

I wrestle with weeds. I wrestle with my irritation over having to weed. But I weed, even when I don't want to. The work is required for the garden to reach its full potential. Drawing an analogy to the Jacob-Esau story, weeds are the permanent and inevitable limp that shows up in every garden. The weeds must be acknowledged and dealt with. Denial is not an option if the garden is going to have any chance to flourish.

As a country, we have wrestled with race and racism for centuries. The wrestling has left us, all of us, of any race or ethnicity, with a cultural limp. It is our historical legacy. The limp is existential, yet it can manifest itself in physical, psychological, and spiritual ways. Our limps are different, depending on race, history, or circumstance; some are crippling, some are barely noticeable. Whenever it came, and however it manifests itself, we each have inherited a limp that requires our attention. Now there are many, particularly among those of us who live in the dominant American culture, who say, "I don't have a limp, especially from my wrestling with race . . . because I don't need to wrestle with race . . . it's no longer an issue, with me, anyway . . ." or "I maybe had a limp once, but now it's gone. We just need to get over it."

I have made some of those statements. As one whose lineage makes both subtle and overt claims to a racial birthright, I was able to delude myself into thinking that I didn't need to wrestle with race. For most of my adolescence, I lived in a well-to-do, virtually all-white community. Race was outside our borders, and was not welcomed in. There were some very carefully organized wrestling matches on the subject, but they were rather shallow and limited to the theoretical; in my memory no one ever walked away with a limp.

As I grew and began to see more of the world outside that small enclave, I began to see those for whom life had been very different, whose limps were the result of very different fights. My college community wrestled with racial injustice. Openly and directly. It was hard work. We needed to keep at it. I discovered that we all had a limp. There were the limps of those who had long been oppressed, and there were the limps of those who had been the oppressors. There were the limps of those who had truly wrestled, and the limps of those who wrestled to avoid really wrestling.

I began to learn that the American dream, as Ta-Nehisi Coates describes it in *Between the World and Me*, was designed to advance the lives of white people at the expense of opportunities for Black people. Yet there were all sorts of practices and habits that continued to make it difficult for some, like me, to see that our birthright had been stolen from others.

In the privileged Connecticut community where I grew up, most of the mothers I knew volunteered at the annual Children's Aid sale. The women were visibly honored for their work: Each was provided with a colorful apron with their name stitched on the front, which they wore as they sorted and priced and monitored the sale. Items were donated, mostly clothing, by the well-off suburbanites, and sold at considerable discount to people in the neighboring communities, who tended to be economically poorer and physically darker, and the proceeds went to support a local agency that worked with at-risk families. It was a noble enterprise.

Technically, the donated clothes were hand-me-downs, but they usually were simply out of fashion or they were the wrong size. Most everything was in mint condition. My sisters and I looked forward to the annual sale, not because of what we were able to give, but what we could get. The day before the sale opened to the public, the volunteers were given the opportunity to go through the display and buy whatever they wanted for the tag sale price. My mother would come back with a pile of clothes for each of the four of us, having spent a fraction of the cost of buying the clothes at a retail store. Children's Aid outfitted us better than anything else my family could afford to buy at market prices.

I don't think it ever occurred to people that there was some inequity in the system that gave first dibs to the volunteers. There were plenty of left-over leftovers for the public; and besides, it seemed only fair that the donors, sorters, and sellers should have first crack. It wasn't an issue that anyone thought to wrestle with; to consider whether it might not be fairer for the volunteers to have free rein over the merchandise after the public sale rather than before it. But the dynamics of the Children's Aid sale, like so many other "noble enterprises," while offering a welcome service, nevertheless reinforced the concept of a birthright. Most of those on the donating and volunteering end were not able to see it. I certainly wasn't.

The realities of white security and birthright privilege make it difficult to say that the limp white people carry is real and permanent. So many live with the notion that this limp can be wished or willed away, a denial of the racial prejudice that everyone has learned or inherited. If there is an original sin, it is our prejudice, our inability to see our common belovedness. We all learned it—at the kitchen table or on the playground or in the school cafeteria, or from skewed readings of the Bible—or in church. We all learned it. To deny our prejudice, our limp, is self-deception. There are some genealogists who make the case that this prejudice is bred into us. It is our inherent limp. It is the weed of original sin that keeps cropping up in the garden of life, threatening the fragile nature of the garden's harmony and undermining our integrity.

When I took an anti-racism course nearly twenty years ago, I discovered that my first exposure to prejudice was not so much about race as it was about religion (which turned out to be a variation of race). From age three to ten I lived in Glencoe, Illinois, a town just north of Chicago on Lake Michigan that was eighty percent Jewish. I learned of Yom Kippur because it was the day in the school year when I was one of two or three people in my classroom; all the Jewish kids were somewhere else. In the late 1950s there was never a consideration of declaring the Day of Atonement a school holiday. Quite the contrary. During Advent, I remember the entire elementary school gathering in the auditorium at the beginning of the school day to sing Christmas carols. I loved to sing, and especially to sing those songs; but I was completely oblivious to the fact that the carols were foreign, if not offensive, to my Jewish classmates. Many years later I surmised that the annual Advent carol singing was a form of religious harassment. It was yet another example of demonstrating birthright.

Religious prejudice was reinforced by the fact that although I lived in a predominantly Jewish town, my neighborhood was mostly Christian. Many of the neighborhood kids went to a Catholic school in the next town. So I had two sets of friends: the kids from school and the kids in the neighborhood. I heard anti-Semitic slurs in the neighborhood, and from my paternal grandfather. But they were, for the most part, contained within the Christian silos where I spent my non-school time.

Except when they weren't. One incident stands out. It was early summer after my third or fourth grade year. I was walking with two school friends, Lee and Mitch, both of whom were Jewish, after playing baseball on the school field. We were headed to Mitch's house. A few blocks from his home we came across two kids who lived on the next block from me. I didn't know them very well; we had played baseball and kick-the-can a few times. They were a year or two older than me and attended the parochial school in the next town. They said a quick hello to me, and before I could respond to their greeting, they proceeded to violently beat up Mitch and Lee. It happened so quickly that I couldn't figure out what to say or do. I could see what was going on, but I couldn't figure out why.

When we got to Mitch's house, we were met by his father, a big bear of a man whom I had met before. And he was furious—at me. Because I didn't do anything.

It took me awhile, several years probably, before I was able to see that the beating of my friends was anti-Semitism in action. It took me many years more to realize that I had absorbed the anti-Semitic slurs from the neighborhood, my grandfather, and elsewhere—and while I can't say that I believed the slurs, I can't say that I disbelieved them; that at some deep level I felt I carried the birthright of religious (if not racial) primacy.

And I hadn't done anything when Mitch and Lee were attacked. Because at some deep, buried in the gut level, as a nine- or ten-year-old I believed that the beating was simply reinforcing the natural order of things. I have spent most of my adult life working at un-believing that. It is a weed that crops up. It is a wrestling that I need to engage in, that has left me with a lifelong spiritual limp.

The weeds of anti-Semitism were the first weeds I identified. But other weeds have sprouted up—racial discrimination, homophobia, misogyny, class distinction. I have had to learn where they have come from, what life circumstances (notably anxiety and fear) prompt their growth—and what weeding I need to do. I have had moments, if not seasons, of reconciliation, but they have been fragile. I need to keep working at it.

We are not told why it was that Jacob sought reconciliation with his brother. The text infers that after decades and amassing a fortune of livestock, servants, and slaves and having produced a large family, Jacob had a certain legitimacy about him and felt he was no longer a renegade. I wonder if there was a more primal desire: Jacob wanted to be blessed. Not a contrived or deceitful blessing, but an honest blessing. Jacob was willing to abjectly humble himself to receive his brother's blessing.

In American history we have countless examples of deceitful blessings: the blessings of redacted history, the blessings of deceitful transactions, the blessings of false narratives and stolen birthrights.

The weeds of the original sin of racism can be met by God's blessing, which is always offered. It is an original blessing. It produces fragile reconciliations in a diverse, often disruptive world. The blessing is effective only if we, like Jacob, humble ourselves and rid ourselves of our pride and arrogance and recognize our prejudice, risking exposure to God's judgment (which requires us to be honest with our story) along with his blessing and mercy. God keeps working at blessing us. We need to keep working at weeding our prejudice, practicing humility, and recognizing our limp. Not to deny it, avoid it, or store it away on some psychic shelf but to see it as fully as is humanly possible, so we can authentically reconcile with others.

And then, and only then, can we be faithful stewards of this blessing and share it with a world that desperately needs it.

FINDING MANDORLA SPACE IN THE GUN DEBATE

I have never owned a gun. As far as I know, very few of my friends own guns. I did a little bit of shooting at an outdoor firing range with a .22 rifle when I was a Boy Scout, but that was nearly sixty years ago. I don't remember much, except that a lot of time was spent on gun safety instruction.

I have had little relationship with guns. And little, if any, relationship with people who owned guns. But in recent years I have had a very engaged relationship with the gun debate. It began when a bishop colleague called me and asked if I would be willing to work with him on reducing gun violence. I said I would and offered to enlist the commitment of two other colleagues. They agreed, and the four of us, from Milwaukee, Newark, Chicago, and Baltimore—cities that had alarming levels of gun violence—began to have some conversations about how we could employ our roles as bishops to help reduce the scourge.

Then, on December 14, 2012, Sandy Hook happened. Twenty children and six teachers were murdered by a mentally disturbed young man, who had broken into the school armed with semiautomatic weapons. Within two weeks we had a network of bishops from across the country who were motivated to do what we could to reduce gun violence. We formed a network called Bishops United Against Gun Violence, raised some money from our cohort, started a website, hired a public relations/administration company, and developed a strategy of education, advocacy, and public witness. Over the years we have grown to a network of one hundred bishops. We lobby locally and nationally, we write op-eds, we have made public witness in Washington, DC, and Chicago—as well as at our triennial General Conventions of the Episcopal Church in Salt Lake City, Utah, and Austin, Texas. When I retired from active ministry in October 2018, I became the bishop liaison to other groups working in the gun violence prevention field. I joined weekly phone calls with representatives from the Brady Campaign, Giffords (named after Representative Gabrielle Giffords, who was shot in the head in 2011), Everytown for Gun Safety, Moms Demand Action, March for Our Lives (which emerged out of the Parkland, Florida, shooting on February 14, 2018), the Center for American Progress, Physicians against Gun Violence, Newtown Action Alliance, Community Justice Action Fund (working with Black and brown communities to end gun violence), States United, and a host of others. My role has been to develop partnerships between our bishops' group and others working in the gun violence prevention movement.

I am grateful for the relationships I have established outside the church through this work, and the knowledge that I have gained from them. I have learned about the escalation of gun violence in the United States—from ninety deaths a day four years ago to over one hundred in

2019. I have learned that suicide is the cause of over sixty percent of gun deaths in the US, and even higher in states with less stringent gun laws (nearly ninety percent of gun deaths in New Hampshire are by suicide). I have learned that there are an estimated 4.5 million children in America who live in homes with unsecured firearms, which is a prescription for unintended injury or death. The list could go on and on.

And I have learned more about the other side of the gun control debate. They are well funded, organized, and passionate. As solidarity and commitment grew among the gun violence prevention community, so too did an antipathy toward the other side. Any notion of seeing gun rights activists in their own humanity was lost; their views needed to be defeated. They were the adversary.

In late 2019 I was invited to participate in a four-person online debate sponsored by Braver Angels, a national movement and organization that seeks to depolarize America, as discussed earlier. Two of us were gun violence prevention people and two were gun rights people. In true debate fashion, I worked on my three-minute presentation. I was somewhat conciliatory in my remarks, but not much. And as soon as I heard the arguments from the other side, my competitive instincts kicked in. I wanted to win. I am not proud of this competitive, zero-sum posture, but there it was. Martin Luther King Jr. often said that the goal of the civil rights movement was not victory but reconciliation. I got that conceptually, but in the throes of our debate the commitment to reconciliation was nowhere to be found.

My next visceral response was arrogance. Not only did I want to win, but as the "conversation" continued, I felt ever stronger that not only was I right, but that the other side was wrong. I listened not for valid points made by the other side but for the holes in their arguments, the inaccuracy of their data, and the overall weakness of their position. My arrogance was at full throttle.

This wasn't the first time. About twenty years ago I participated in a daylong facilitated conversation with a group of colleagues on the issue of homosexuality. It was then a very charged issue and both sides were represented at the event. A few hours in, I reacted to a colleague who was a friend and someone I trusted, despite our differences of opinion. I told him that I thought a particular statement he made was arrogant. Without missing a beat, he said that he had spent the whole day trying to ignore my arrogance, and after hearing my comment he said that he had had it. It took each of us awhile to acknowledge and then own our respective arrogance—and when we did, a real conversation began, because we were no long posturing or angling for the best position. Only when we were able to acknowledge our respective arrogance were we able to really listen to one another. I credit the skill of the facilitator and our mutual respect with enabling us to move from a debate posture to actual conversation, to a place where we could actually see one another in our humanity.

At the gun debate, my ultimate, and perhaps most troubling, visceral response was fear. My arrogance may still have been in play here because I could see, hear, and feel the fear on the other side: The fear that guns would be taken away; the fear that the Second Amendment would be violated; the fear that federal, state, or local officials were not up to the task of protecting them; the fear of an intruder coming into their homes intending bodily harm.

But my fear? I feared for kids in schools, I feared for young Black men and mentally ill people who are being scapegoated as the sources of gun violence. I feared for the proliferation of guns, which produces more violence. But that is displaced fear—it is fear *for*. Fear *of* is different. I think my real fear was not of guns but of the positions and attitudes held so passionately by those in the gun rights community. They scared me. Their certainty and arrogance frightened me, as did the anger that is so palpable behind them.

As I talk to people who convey a passionate support for gun rights and the Second Amendment, they express a similar fear: That their rights will be taken away by people who have no understanding of and experience with guns. People who show no respect for guns, unlike their fellow gun owners who take great care in the storage and use of firearms. We end up fearing the "other" not on the basis of how they look or where they live but out of what we think they believe.

Increasingly, the cultural norm is to respond to one another with fear, which is usually masked with arrogance and a façade of certainty.

My attitude shifted a bit when I attended the annual American Association of Suicidology Conference in April 2019. The issue of gun suicide was not a concept I had thought much about, and I wanted to learn from people who worked in the field. Several thousand people from all over the country attended the conference, many of whom had been working in the suicide prevention arena for years. They were passionate about saving lives, and were concerned about the rapid increase in suicide, especially among teenagers.

By chance I happened to meet the co-chair of a suicide task force on the West Coast. She was on a university faculty, with a specialization in social work. Her husband had taken his life with a gun several years before. She was engaged personally and professionally in reducing suicide. I talked about my developing relationships in the gun violence prevention movement. She firmly but graciously asked me not to use that term, because the gun rights people in her network, who were just as committed to reducing gun suicide as she was, were turned off by it. "It sounds too social science-y," she said. "Gun violence prevention" carries with it an arrogance and self-righteousness that come across as judgmental and undermine the ability to work together across different attitudes about guns. She said that what was most important was to develop relationships between gun owners and mental health professionals. She said that the group with which she worked had effectively done that: While it took a long time for both sides to build up trust, they were able to learn from and respect one another. She told me that a senior member of the National Rifle Association was enormously helpful in crafting legislation and establishing a process that involved both sides of the gun issue—and was saving lives.

Suicide by guns is a growing tragedy. There are dozens of safety coalitions across the country, where gun shop owners and mental health professionals work together to educate the public about the incidence of gun suicide and to reduce it. A group in New Hampshire formed the first coalition about a dozen years ago, and their example has been replicated in many other parts of the country. Through the building of relationships, which in turn fostered respect and trust, these coalitions have been able to bridge the cultural divide on guns and work together toward the goal of saving lives.

The dedicated people who had been working for years in the arena of suicide prevention exposed my own arrogance and self-righteousness with respect to the gun culture, which, quite frankly, I knew nothing about. I knew their arguments, but I didn't know the culture.

So I went to a gun show. The hotel ballroom where it was held was filled with guns, knives, holsters, ammunition, and all sorts of accessories. Most of the booths sold antique guns, some of which dated back to the Revolutionary War. A couple of nineteenth-century rifles had price tags in excess of $20,000. There was a continuous flow of mostly men coming into the show, handling the merchandise, and occasionally making a purchase. And there was talking, lots of talking, between the vendors and shoppers, among the shoppers, and with the representatives from the NRA foundation and local gun clubs.

And I listened. In truth, I eavesdropped—and hoped that people wouldn't recognize me as an outlier, which I certainly was. In very short order I realized that the language these men used quite comfortably was language I didn't understand. I had very little idea of what they were talking about. But I could certainly see and hear the passion. The passion was real, and it was deep—and the gun show was a safe place where they could claim an identity that had a long history and that was uniquely American. On the surface, their identity was about guns, but it was deeper than that; the vendors and shoppers were part of an American culture that is not easily acknowledged and is often misunderstood. And it is a culture that is not going to go away. Guns have been in America since Europeans settled on this continent, claiming it as their own, using guns at every step of western expansion to kill for food, to protect livestock from predators—and more than occasionally to kill or subdue whoever blocked the path of manifest destiny. The history of guns in America has many layers. An insistent inner voice wants to

dodge part of this history, or at least remove the weapons of destruction from its telling. That inner voice is shared by millions of others
who claim to be advocates of peace. This desire to view our history minus guns is what gun rights advocates fear—that the gun disdainers
will try and take away their guns and the culture in which guns are an
integral part.

It is a vicious cycle—of arrogance and self-righteousness on one
side, and defensiveness and armed defense on the other. How to bridge
the chasm?

I took a gun class. I wanted to know more about gun culture, with
the hope that more knowledge would somehow help me bridge the
chasm. I was there to learn; most everyone else was there to receive a
training certificate that would enable them to get a gun permit from the
local police department and then purchase a firearm.

I learned several things in the half-day Saturday class. The first
was—this is complicated. At the beginning of the class the instructor, a
retired police detective, had us each come up and pick up a plastic hand-
gun, which had the exact shape and heft of a 9-millimeter pistol. After
each of us had picked it up and pointed it at a target, the instructor told
us that he would have been shot in the stomach by at least half the class,
because we had picked up the weapon incorrectly and had our finger on
the trigger before pointing it at the target. It could have fired. As the
lesson progressed and we were instructed in how to hold, aim, and shoot
the pistol with the proper sequence of thumb position, safety release, and
pointing, I couldn't keep it all straight. I was so distracted by the time it
was my turn to fire my five rounds in the firing range that I had no idea
where the bullet went, nor did I care.

At the end of the class, I received my certificate, which gave me permission to own and carry a gun. A scary thought, as I had gained no competence in using it from that Saturday morning class.

There were sixteen others in the class—an equal number of males and females—plus the instructor. But within the first hour a seventeenth showed up. "When Billy Badass, standing six-foot-four, comes at you with a two-by-four in one hand and a machete in the other, you only have a few seconds to shoot him down," the instructor said. I waved the image off. But the instructor brought him up again, and Billy Badass came into the room and never left. This menacing image of a badass of an unnamed race (although I felt the implication was clear) was a strong motivation for people to take the course.

It all made me deeply sad. The guns that my classmates were intending to purchase were violent responses to perceived violence. I was sad that people felt that the only option to the possibility of violence was violence. And I was sad that I felt so separated from people who felt such a strong need to arm themselves.

I had a similar feeling of sadness nearly a year later when I participated in a Zoom Second Amendment debate sponsored by Braver Angels. There were about three hundred and fifty participants, and we were broken up into chat rooms of about eighty each. The debate chair made it clear that we were to engage in the issue with respect and civility. People volunteered to speak, and after short speeches (up to four minutes) questions were invited. Speakers rotated between pro and con. The process served to keep the focus on the arguments and not on the speaker, and in that sense served to mitigate against personal attacks and disruptive behavior.

I fitfully listened to the pro Second Amendment arguments: that the Second Amendment provided people an inalienable right to own guns, which was distinct from actually using guns; that guns were "the great equalizer," in that a gun would emasculate the power of a home intruder. One person said that wealthy people can pay for their protection, but people of modest means needed to be able to protect themselves. An older white man said that there were groups out there who were committed to doing away with people who looked like him and that he needed to be prepared for the assault. Nearly every argument was framed in the context that it was just a matter of time before someone would break into their homes with a gun, the police would never be able to respond in time—and so they needed to arm themselves and shoot when necessary.

Nearly a year earlier, at another event, when I was on a team of two debating the issue of guns, I had focused on my primary argument and rebuttals to the opposition's positions. This debate was different. It was not a contest; it invited listening. Initially, I couldn't believe the arguments I was hearing. How could they really believe that? I felt self-righteous in my reactions. But as time went on, it became clear to me that the Second Amendment proponents really believed what they said. They were passionate about their beliefs. I began to realize that their support for the Second Amendment under any and all circumstances was a foundational component of their identity, much as my challenge to the universality of the Second Amendment was a key dimension of mine.

I wasn't ready to give up my position, or the passion with which I held it; in some ways both were reinforced by the conversation. But the process, and the care with which it was designed and facilitated, brought me beyond our differences to a new realization of our common humanity: We all cared about this. All of us were advocating for greater safety, even though we widely disagreed on the definition of safety and how to achieve it. There was a quality of respect to it that could easily have gone unnoticed. Each of the three hundred plus people who participated harbored some commitment to arrive at that place of common humanity—otherwise they wouldn't have agreed to join in the first place. After all, the fundamental goal of Braver Angels is to depolarize America by appealing to the better angels of our nature.

Quite unexpectedly, for me anyway, the Second Amendment debate brought me, for a moment at least, into the mandorla—that almond-shaped intersection between the circles of the gun rights and gun violence prevention people. I was surprised to find myself in that place; and even found myself concerned that I was betraying my argument and the scores of people I was aligned with who shared the gun violence prevention commitment.

I am still appalled by the proliferation of guns, the escalating rates of gun suicide, and the undiminished commitment of some gun rights advocates to thwart any legislation that calls for more background checks and fewer (if any) semiautomatic weapons. And I will continue to join with others in our advocacy and witness to change those realities. Arguments need to be made, pressure needs to be brought, legislation needs to be enacted.

At the same time, there is the disquieting realization that the arguments and advocacy also have the effect of hardening the positions and hearts on the other side, with the result being, if not a political stalemate, then certainly a spiritual one. We retreat into our circles of safety, if not certainty, and can't imagine or entertain the possibility of common ground. Somehow, and I think Braver Angels is on to something here, there needs to be a process and willingness to see across difference and disagreement for lasting change to occur. Braver Angels sets up debates, workshops, and conversations, not for the purpose of changing minds, but to create space that allows individuals to see beyond arguments to an appreciation of our common humanity. It doesn't always happen, arguments and egos often get in the way, but the combination of intention, hope, and forbearance can make it possible.

12

FINDING MANDORLA
SPACES IN OUR WORK

From the moment I was consecrated as bishop of the Episcopal Diocese of Newark on January 27, 2007, I was bequeathed a raft of protocols, procedures, and responsibilities—not to mention a new wardrobe and identity—that was more extensive, encompassing, and daunting than anything I had ever experienced in my nearly thirty years as a parish priest. For the next twelve years, until my retirement from that position in late September 2018, I strove to learn the protocols and procedures and stay on top of the responsibilities that seemed to metastasize by the week. There is certainly a uniqueness to the identity and role of being a bishop in the Episcopal Church, but there are also common threads and patterns that any leader faces when put in charge of a large organization. I quickly discovered that "seeing" a parish is qualitatively and quantitatively different from "seeing" a diocese with one hundred congregations. For one, the pedestal that many clergy and laypeople put the bishop on is loftier, and the role is conceived to be more regal (a bishop's purple shirt makes a direct connection to royalty), making the distance between bishop and everyone else greater and the projections by others onto a bishop more frequent.

At a bishop's ordination and consecration service, the soon-to-be bishop is subject to a public examination, involving a series of questions that date back hundreds of years (with some slight modifications). It is less a test and more of a pledge, given that the answers are printed. There is one question that has long loomed larger for me than the others (and, as I have heard from many of my colleagues, for them as well): "Will you guard the faith, unity, and discipline of the Church?" (the 1979 Book of Common Prayer, page 518). The scripted response: "I will, for the love of God."

That is a tall order, and an enormous responsibility.

In many ways, for a bishop to be a guardian of the faith is to assume the role of a sentry, which then introduces a wide array of challenges: Where should the sentry be posted? Is the sentry one who encourages people and ideas to come in, or is the sentry one who strives to keep people and ideas out?

What is the bishop expected to see—or choose not to see?

Bishops have different tolerances, and therefore different thresholds for what is to be let in or kept out: what they see and what they ignore. Whatever the tolerance and threshold a single bishop may adopt, or the community of bishops establish, there will be those who will support them, challenge them, complain about them, and be co-dependent upon them.

And so, we wrestle—bishops with bishops, bishops with clergy, clergy with laypeople, laypeople with one another—all in the interest of fostering the faith, unity, and discipline of the church.

When disagreement hits, the wrestling can become a mismatch. The stress can be a real or perceived threat, and the temptation for the bishop is to come down hard: To seal the borders and keep things out. To execute male power and prerogative (most bishops, even if not male, have nevertheless inherited a male-dominant posture that has strongly influenced church systems). In these moments, what we are able to see is the rules and the theology that supports the rules, rather than those who are struggling with issues of faith, unity, and discipline. As a new bishop, I was surprised by how many people looked upon the office of bishop as a regulatory agency. They wanted to know the rules, worried about breaking the rules, and sought, with some exceptions, to comply with the rules. There was a kind of perverse harmony in this dynamic: It kept us distant from one another and reduced my role to that of an ecclesiastical referee. Being a guardian of the faith is very different from exploring the faith together.

As a priest, I broke the rules, particularly when it came to offering Communion to people who had not yet been baptized. It has long been the practice in the Episcopal Church to offer Communion only to communicants of the church, which refers to people who have been baptized. Baptism is the port of entry to receiving Communion.

For many years I respected that boundary. I would not give Communion to people who had not been baptized. That was challenged one day when a single mother with her three young children returned to the Episcopal church where I served as rector and where she had grown up. For several weeks she brought them to the rail with her. I gave her Communion and blessed her kids. As we got to know one another she asked why I didn't give them Communion. "Because they hadn't been baptized," I responded (knowing that the family had been adherents of the Nation of Islam). "It's not their fault," she quickly retorted. She challenged my threshold, and because of her I moved it. From that day on, I gave Communion to anyone who desired it. I invoked the invitation from the Church of St. Gregory of Nyssa in San Francisco: "All who seek God and are drawn to Christ are welcome at the Lord's table." My invitation challenged the rubrics of the church, but the mother's challenge to me outweighed my adherence to the ecclesiastical rules.

I brought that commitment and conviction to the Diocese of Newark when I became bishop, but I was a little more careful in my invitation because I knew there were clergy whose threshold for Communion was different than mine. I wanted to honor their faith and discipline, thinking it unfair to demand that they follow my practice and embrace my theology.

Some clergy in the diocese were very worried. They were, in faith, disposed to offer Communion to people who hadn't yet been baptized, but they knew they were breaking the rules if they did so. "What happens if I'm brought up on charges?," they asked with no small amount of anxiety, concerned that someone, somewhere would raise official questions about their actions. Would I have their backs?

Would I be with them—see them—in their faithful struggle—or simply revert to being the chief steward of the regulatory agency?

It took several years of wrestling with the issue and one another to develop trust and establish a new way of being with one another. Over the course of time, I began to see myself less as a guardian of the faith and more of a gardener in the faith. Less of a sentry and more of a steward. Planting seeds, nurturing growth—and engaging in the never-ending task of pulling weeds. Most of the time, clergy and congregations were eager for the support when the bishop's office offered its presence, program, and wisdom. And most of the time clergy and congregations were willing to identify the weeds—be it conflict, misbehavior, financial challenges, or impropriety—and held out hope that we could work together in removing them. Occasionally it fell to me as bishop to identify weeds that others didn't see or would refuse to recognize, and then go about the daunting task of pulling them.

Issues were more complex and positions more deeply entrenched on the national level. I entered the episcopate as the Episcopal Church was in the throes of dealing with human sexuality. The issue had been brewing for years and came to a head in the 2003 election of Gene Robinson as the bishop of New Hampshire. A partnered gay man, Gene's consecration set off a resistance movement that was filled with more anger and hurt (not to mention a proliferation of theological treatises) than had surfaced earlier around this issue. I would like to say that as bishops we wrestled with the issue, but it felt more like open combat. Many maintained that Gene's consecration was a weed that needed to be removed; some even made the case that Gene himself was a weed (he wore a Kevlar vest under his vestments at his consecration to protect himself because of the death threats he received). I was part of a growing majority who felt that Gene and his consecration was a blessing and gift to the church.

Lines were drawn. It was hard for bishops to see the other position or to seek the common mandorla ground, given the intensity of the anger and hurt. The Anglican Communion, of which the Episcopal Church is a part and which has 75 million adherents around the world, was deeply divided. At a 2008 gathering of Episcopal and Anglican bishops from around the world (minus a few hundred who refused to come because

the American Church had consecrated Gene Robinson), the official purpose was to reinforce collegiality and promote common mission, but the
issue of human sexuality seeped into every conversation and created a
polarized atmosphere. At one point, the gathering, numbering about one
thousand people, was addressed by Jonathan Sacks, the chief rabbi in
England at the time and a scholar of remarkable talent. He told us that
he had grown up attending Anglican schools, and so he knew all about
our tradition. He went on to say that we were one of the largest volunteer organizations in the world, if not the largest. And he said—no, he
shouted—you have to stay together, for the sake of the rest of us. If you
fall apart, he thundered, it would be catastrophic for other sects, groups,
and federations that, like the Anglican Communion, were held together
by "bonds of affection."

Those bonds of affection nearly snapped. Some may argue that they
already have. But what I learned from the three-week experience of being with 700 bishops from around the world is that the depth and length
of relationships—of years of connection with one another across cultures,
races, and traditions—were deeper and more abiding than differences in
theology. Beneath it all we mattered to one another.

Over the course of the next several years, from my perspective at
least, the Anglican Communion and the Episcopal Church (which is a
province within the Anglican Communion) moved from open combat
to supervised wrestling. From wanting to destroy the opponent, to being willing to go to the mat with the other side, with both coming out
whole. From being sentries who were always standing at the ready to
guard against intrusion or prevent escape, to serving as stewards who
sought to identify and strengthen bonds of affection.

The wrestling continues. Some are still intent on engaging in combat, although much of it has gone underground. Some have simply given up and have either left or disappeared. It was hard and it was painful. It still is. But the lines are no longer as sharply drawn; there is a growing openness and willingness to listen to one another, seeing one another as children of God trying to do the best we can.

How we view one another takes on an entirely different dimension when a bishop is legally and ethically bound to engage in a process that involves the accusation, investigation, and adjudication of clergy accused of misconduct. Guarding the faith becomes a time-consuming and heart-wrenching engagement for everyone involved. In my twelve years as bishop, involving twelve cases of misconduct, the protocols that had been researched, debated, and enacted over the years by the General Convention of the Episcopal Church (which is the triennial legislative meeting of bishops, elected clergy, and laypeople), placed the bishop as a sentry to protect the safety and integrity of the church from the alleged transgression of clergy. It is a daunting responsibility. At the first seminar/workshop I attended for bishops on the matter, led by a lawyer who had a hand in drafting the comprehensive and lengthy protocol, she remarked that the outline is complex but clear—and that we had to get it right. Being careless, cavalier, or unclear can wreak havoc on the accused priest, his or her congregation, and on the wider church.

The first challenge for me as bishop when the first accusation was raised was to read, learn, mark, and inwardly digest the protocol. To sit with it. To see how it works, what it is meant to do. To discover a rhythm for working with the appropriate colleagues— the chancellor, intake officer, and head of the review panel for the process.

The next challenge was to fully embrace the accusation. This was perhaps the most difficult aspect: To acknowledge the possibility of such a breach of trust and breaking of boundaries, the verbal violence or sexual transgression. Clergy take vows to be wholesome examples to their people (Book of Common Prayer, page 532). But people break their vows or act out of stupidity or narcissism or frustration or fear.

In her recent book, *Holy Envy: Finding Faith in the Lives of Others*, author and Episcopal priest Barbara Brown Taylor makes a distinction between pain and suffering. Pain, she writes, is the response to hurt, loss, sadness, grief. Suffering is a feeling compounded onto pain by the desire that it wasn't there to begin with, or that the pain would go away, or the conviction that it is unfair. Suffering intensifies pain; it is real, and understandable. As I struggled to acknowledge each accusation of misconduct, I strove to see the pain within the situation unclouded by my own dismayed suffering. Of all the responsibilities I had as bishop, overseeing misconduct accusations carried the most authority—and had the most impact on a priest or a church.

It was not easy. It was always painful.

It was at times tempting to see my role as limited to being a sentry, and to invoke a heavy-handed approach, allowing myself emotional and spiritual distance from the process. But I soon learned that these processes provided an opportunity to serve as steward of a sacred trust. There was a pastoral dimension to the process, caring for the accused, the complainant, and all those involved while honoring confidentiality and privacy requirements.

"I will be with you," God said to Moses and to Joshua. "I will be with you," Jesus said to his disciples. That certainly was my mantra, if not my prayer, as my team and I went through the cases that were presented to us. And I suspect it was the mantra and prayer of others who were accused and affected by the onerous challenges wrought by such cases.

"I will be with you" may not be a solution to vexing issues, but it offers an enormous help in working through them. And in a subtle way, it is an invitation to look beyond the challenges and conflicts and see the promise of divine presence. We can find blessing in the midst of injustice.

13

INSTITUTIONAL SIGHTLINES

For a society to sustain itself, it needs institutions. Schools, hospitals, businesses, shops, factories, religious sanctuaries—places where people are employed to teach, heal, sell, build, and worship. Places where products are made and services are offered for the purpose of maintaining the commonwealth and community welfare. Places that both feed the market economy and the economy of human flourishing.

Some institutions have less to do with that economy of human flourishing, and yet they have developed to serve society. I am thinking of those institutions whose purpose it is to remove people from the rest of society—prisons, nursing homes, mental hospitals, juvenile detention centers, and the like; ostensibly for the residents' (or inmates') protection, care, and, in some cases, rehabilitation. Prisons are formally referred to as houses of correction, which suggests that those who are incarcerated will have their criminal behavior identified, addressed, and corrected by the time they reenter society. Nursing homes are often identified as long-term care facilities; their names often include images of sunshine, havens, and hope.

We need these and other institutions. But their existence—and particularly the terminology we use for them—indicates that who is really being protected and cared for is the rest of society. It doesn't take much research to determine that "correctional facility" is a misnomer for prisons. They are widely regarded as citadels of punishment, which a substantial portion of the population feels that inmates deserve. As for nursing homes, they are too often where people in their last months or years are sent to die. In these and other cases, these institutions exist so that their prisoners or residents don't have to be seen.

Prior to the 1970s, state mental hospitals fit this model. Mentally ill people who were clinically determined to be at risk to themselves or others were remanded to secure facilities, sometimes for years. When phenothiazines began to be administered to psychotic patients in the early 1970s, inaugurating a psychiatric drug revolution, a flood of medicated patients, no longer requiring in-patient care, were released to their local communities, which rarely had the capacity to receive them. Community mental health centers were established, but there were too few of them, often underfunded, and they were overwhelmed by the surge in cases.

So mentally ill people began to hang out on the streets, suddenly a visible part of society. The homeless crisis, which began to crescendo in the early 1980s, was often blamed on the "de-institutionalization" of mental hospitals, although economic issues were far more influential in generating homelessness. No matter. Mentally ill people were easy to blame. As the homeless crisis deepened, communities, congregations, and civic groups worked together to create shelters, generate funding, and offer services, but it wasn't enough. Alongside these efforts, there was an equal, if not larger, response to the growing problem of homelessness—which was to get homeless people off the streets. Out of sight and out of mind. Their presence was considered an affront to a well-run society.

When I arrived at Norwich State Hospital in Connecticut in 1978 as a chaplain resident, what had been an expansive campus filled with over two thousand patients was then down to fewer than seven hundred. There were boarded-up buildings, scaled-back programs, and skeleton staffs. Except for the drug and alcohol treatment center, every ward was locked. *One Flew over the Cuckoo's Nest*, a popular 1975 movie about a state mental hospital based on the 1962 Ken Kesey novel of the same name, featured a malevolent hospital staff at odds (or at war) with a hyperkinetic, anti-social patient. While the film was a bit exaggerated in its depiction of life on a locked mental ward, in many ways I found the movie to be congruent with my yearlong experience in a similar facility. Norwich Hospital had its challenges, to be sure, but it also had a fragile culture, created by the patients who resided there, that offered support and care.

We need institutions. They provide grounding and a function within society. And because institutions inevitably focus on self-preservation, they need continual reform, which requires commitment, work—and a lot of time.

Years ago, in the middle of a Martin Luther King Day sermon, the Rev. Dr. James Washington, professor of modern and American Church history at Union Theological Seminary in New York, asked the congregation a supposedly rhetorical question: "Do you know what a liberal is?" he politely queried. The congregation, which was almost entirely Black, knew the answer, but was more than eager for Dr. Washington to answer it himself. "A liberal," he went on, "is someone who approaches a house infested with termites. The liberal then takes a splinter out of the house—and fumigates it." He stretched out the last part. "The liberal then takes the now insect-free splinter, looks at his good work, puts it back in the house, and goes home."

The congregation stood and cheered. They knew this story. Most had been on the receiving end of it more times than they could count.

Too often, we who call ourselves liberals condition ourselves to see only a corner of a problem or an issue. We address that small corner, but nominally, and with enough self-satisfaction to keep our vision truncated. Mission trips, organized by civic, educational, or religious groups, send people to economically (and often politically) challenged areas of the world (or in our own country) to experience firsthand the poverty and degradation of a place foreign to their experience. Work is done, relationships are built, encounters are reflected upon—and then people go home. In his book *Toxic Charity*, Robert Lupton describes mission sites in Central and South America where groups come down for a week and paint a building. Several times during the mission season, a group will come down and repaint the same building, all in the interest of doing mission.

I have known mission trip alumni who told me that their horizons completely changed after such a journey. That the experience taught them to see places and situations of degradation and oppression that they hadn't noticed before and to engage in their communities in new ways. But for most mission trippers, they come back to a comparatively safe and comfortable environment, and their distant experience remains just that—distant. They fumigated a splinter and returned home.

A worldwide institutional reform movement emerged in the wake of the 2008 Great Recession. A Million Man March on Wall Street was organized in February 2011, to protest income disparity and expose the injustice of the top one percent of wealth earners, who were accused of reaping enormous financial benefits at the expense of the remaining 99 percent. The march was not particularly successful, but their next step garnered media attention, and their message spread across the world. The marchers stayed, and occupied Wall Street. The Occupy movement attracted hundreds of other protesters who joined the encampment in Zuccotti Park in lower Manhattan. Some seven hundred similar encampments sprang up in solidarity all over the world. Their clarion call was "We are the 99 percent," and their grievances were blared across the airwaves and social media: Forgive student loan debt, stop the foreclosure machine, and reform banking by ending predatory lending (a major factor in the Great Recession), all in aid of a more equitable and balanced economy. The movement allowed many to envision a new model of economic equity.

One of the creators of Occupy Wall Street, Micah White, wrote a book, *The End of Protest*, that reflected on the protest's achievements and shortcomings. On one hand, White writes, the protest was enormously successful, in that the original New York action was replicated all over the world. And the slogans "We are the 99 percent" and "Challenge the one percent" outlived the many occupations and provided focus for future work. On the other hand, White continued, the protests played right into the hands of the one percent, who were nervously content to allow the protest to play out, figuring that their occupiers' commitment would eventually wane, and people would leave. Let them blow off steam, the thinking went, and when the steam is gone, so will their commitment.

Which sort of happened. The police razed the Zuccotti Park encampment in November, and after howls of protest, the occupiers went home. In his book, White indicated that he and others learned from their ten-month protest and needed to incorporate new strategies going forward. They vowed to keep at it.

The Rev. William Sloane Coffin was a veteran protester, whose oratorical and leadership skills brought him to national prominence in both the anti-war movement in the 1960s and 1970s and the nuclear freeze movement in the 1980s. I remember him speaking to a group of us at Yale Divinity School (where he had graduated a few decades before). He talked about protest and protesters. He said, "Seventy to eighty percent of them don't want to win. They want to vent their spleen, feel self-righteous about their anger and sense of injustice. Their protest is a misguided way to work out some unresolved issues in their own lives, and not on the issue at hand."

I have done that. Especially in my younger years, I worked myself up to a high dudgeon over an issue that seemed unjust, joining a group of people whose sense of indignation matched my own. We said and did some things that released my adrenaline, and then moved on. It felt like a great purging, because I was unknowingly working out some deep resentment that may have had only a slender connection with the issue we had identified. I resist reading or posting on social media because I often find them to be platforms for similar expressions: They release a lot of steam, get people worked up—and help to seal people off from one another.

For over two hundred and fifty years in America (and prior to the nation's founding) much of the economy was dependent on the institution of slavery. Much has been said and written about the injustice and cruelty of slavery, and the damage its legacy inflicts on our national life.

The trauma of the institution of slavery continues in the ongoing reality of systemic racism. As a nation, we have long worked to keep separate our vision of our white forebearers and the horrific events in our history. This has become harder to do, especially after the world watched the video of the murder of George Floyd on May 25, 2020. In those nearly ten minutes, the event captured on film couldn't be erased. Interpretations of what happened ran the gamut, but the footage was undeniable. It could not be said that the killing didn't happen; that it couldn't be seen. The trauma of racial injustice and systemic racism was brought to a new level of awareness for white America.

That new level of awareness requires that we see those whose stories are now being told. There are so many stories. Stories of trauma and oppression, personal and raw. These stories come from the soul, are hard to tell, and are infused with pain and vulnerability. Yet when we don't tell or hear these stories, in an effort to keep our distance from pain and vulnerability, we learn not to see the individuals and experiences within them and lose the insights and understandings they have to offer.

Sadly, too many have responded to these stories from the soul with hardened hearts. The ego is resistant to pain and vulnerability. Ego-driven stories are not designed to open us up, or to help us see life in its fullness, but instead to establish ourselves in a pecking order. The ego doesn't want to hear stories that emerge from the soul.

In Matthew's Gospel Jesus tells his disciples a story, actually offering a prediction: That he will be betrayed and will suffer and be killed. Peter's response erupts right out of the ego: "God forbid, Lord. That can never happen to you" (Matthew 16:22). Peter didn't want to hear of the suffering. He tried to deny it. He is not alone.

As Jesus and his entourage are leaving Jericho after leading some first-century seminars, he is approached by Bartimaeus, a blind beggar. "Jesus, son of David, have mercy on me," Bartimaeus shouts (Mark 10:47). Members of the entourage hear Bartimaeus's plea before Jesus does, and they try to have him removed. They don't want to deal with the blind man's trauma, and they don't want Jesus to hear him, worried that he might respond. They have more important things to do. Bartimaeus voices his plea again, this time much louder, and Jesus hears the blind man's request, listens to his story, and responds: "Go; your faith has made you well" (Mark 10:52).

What changes hearts and reforms institutions is the openness to see others and hear their stories. Stories that bring together the event, the people involved, and the memories they produce. Stories that tell what happened and what the impact of the event has been. Stories that invite listening; narratives that have the potential for creating relationships. Stories that allow the listener to see from the storyteller's perspective. These stories provide healing—for both the storyteller and the listener. And if enough of them are told, stories have the capacity to reform institutions.

DARKNESS, DIFFERENCE, AND DELIGHT

During my first year in seminary, I regularly commuted with a classmate to our shared ministry site, a Masonic home for senior citizens, a twenty-minute drive away. She was gifted and committed, and as it turned out, deeply troubled. She made a couple of suicide gestures in her dorm, which concerned her dormmates and raised the attention of the dean's office. After the third attempt, the seminary asked her to leave. I was indignant. How could a seminary community, which prided itself on its Christian foundation, abandon someone who was so talented and so much in need? I had just returned from my two-year stint in Japan, where Christianity was mostly regarded as a curiosity. When I came to seminary, I expected that everyone would be embraced and nurtured by an intentional Christian community. I was soon disappointed.

I took my indignation to the dean. I presented my opinions, trying to mask my moral outrage. My memory of that conversation, some forty-five years ago, is that he mumbled or spoke in double talk. In retrospect, I don't think he said much of anything except to toe the party line. He was certainly uncomfortable with me, but I couldn't tell if he was uncomfortable with the decision the school had made. In my adrenaline-fed arrogant indignation, I found his response unsatisfactory.

In some desperation, I took my concerns to Henri Nouwen, who lived in a basement apartment in the same dorm where my classmate resided. Henri was becoming a nationally, if not internationally, known spiritual giant, but somehow he always made himself available to students. He agreed to meet with me.

I told him the story about my classmate's removal. He said he didn't know much, if anything, about the particulars of the case. When I finished my litany of complaints, I fully expected him to tell me that I had figured the place out, that Christian community was a fiction if not a sham, that I should get out and go to law school and be done with the whole business. Instead, he looked me straight in the eye and said, "What do you expect?"

"More than this," I said. Actually, I am not sure I said anything, too stunned by his response. He went on: people do the best they can, and often it isn't very good. People hurt one another, even when—and often when—they don't intend to. What he didn't say, but certainly implied, was, "Get over it." Not the presumed injustice of the situation, but the fact that people don't behave very well with one another. Get over it, because when you are able to see people in their vulnerability and with their flaws, it becomes paradoxically easier to see people as being imbued with at least a modicum of God's grace. It also cuts down on the ego-driven moral indignation, so that you can deal with the situation with better perspective.

I have told the story about my meeting with Henri dozens of times over the years partly because, no, mainly because, I am trying to get over the fact that people do dark things to one another. Realizing that reality has, over the years, lowered my ego temperature so I can see injustice more clearly and challenge it more effectively.

Most people, particularly those in twelve-step groups, are familiar with the Serenity Prayer: "God give me the serenity to accept the things I cannot change, the courage to change the things I can, and the wisdom to know the difference." What I didn't know until recently is that Reinhold Niebuhr's famous prayer continues: "Living one day at a time, enjoying one moment at a time, accepting hardship as a pathway to peace; taking, as Jesus did, this sinful world as it is, not as I would have it; trusting that You will make all things right if I surrender to Your will; so that I may be reasonably happy in this life, and supremely happy with You forever in the next."

"Taking, as Jesus did, this sinful world as it is, *not as I would have it*": That takes a lot of work—and the work is letting go in order to see what is. Letting go of the expectation that the world be free of darkness. Letting go of our indignation that the darkness exists. The darkness is there; we have to live in it, deal with it, and see the light in the midst of darkness.

Author Anne Lamott has written that "Expectations are resentments that are under construction." Resentment can generate a spiritual and emotional paralysis, which is what I felt those years ago when Santos Garcia showed up outside my New Jersey church as I was preparing a sermon. My resentment was shrouded in self-righteousness, but the darkness of the night matched that of my soul, which at the time I was not able to acknowledge. His hospitality, kindness, and humility toward me offered light. I almost didn't see it, because I was not willing to take the world as it is.

I heard a story recently about a ranger at Adirondack State Park in New York who was called to a campsite by a distraught woman. Apparently, she had carefully laid out her meal on the picnic table. When she went to get something from her car, a bear came, sat down at the table, and began partaking of a free lunch. When the ranger arrived, the woman complained that the bear was eating her food. The ranger responded that the food was no longer hers; it now belonged to the bear. Unwilling to accept this new reality, she insisted that the ranger get rid of the bear, because it was stealing her food: "It's the principle of the thing. This is my campsite," she is reported to have said in arrogance-fueled anger.

My food. My principle. My campsite. The neophyte camper was not able to see the clear difference between the dynamics of the bear's world and her own. The story may seem like a parody, given the obvious difference between the needs of a bear and presumed rights of a camper, but most of us act a version of this scenario out in all sorts of less dramatic ways. When I arrived in Japan after college, I figured that I had accounted for the difference between American and Japanese culture. But when a caustic but courageous university student pointed out how I took advantage of my greater height and English fluency, differences that I couldn't see, it was not unlike my food, my principle, my campsite.

In 1991, after he was beaten during his arrest, Rodney King said to stressed-out America, "Why can't we all just get along?" Why indeed. His plea is well remembered because it speaks to the common desire for people to get along, to live in a semblance of harmony. There is widespread agreement about the desirability of getting along, but superficial agreement can obscure the various means for achieving the goal. We don't want to see the differences in our emotional diets, how our principles are shaped by different experiences and values—and how rigorously we defend our respective campsites.

Rabbi Jonathan Sacks (1948–2020) wrote that a primordial instinct, going back to humanity's tribal past, has caused us to see difference as a threat. The polarization in America has a tribal quality to it, dysfunctional in an age in which our destinies are intertwined. There is an increasing and urgent need to see and honor difference. As our world gets smaller, there is more tension, turmoil, and violence.

Early in the Book of Genesis, people thought that if they built a tower to heaven they could replace God. God got wind of their hubris and knocked the tower down, scattering people to the corners of the earth with different languages so they couldn't understand one another (Genesis 11:1–9). Most scholars maintain that the Tower of Babel story reflects an intention by God for humanity to learn to live with difference. In sharp contrast, the architects of apartheid in South Africa used this story as justification for keeping races and people separate. While other cultures have not been as overt and egregious in keeping people apart, the culture of separation nonetheless remains. When we are separated, we are more easily threatened by difference and comforted by our projections— and more likely to claim that it is my food, my principle, my campsite.

We need to do better. Which brings me to delight.

On Easter morning in 2021, at an outdoor sunrise service at the Cathedral of the Pines in Rindge, New Hampshire, attended by about two hundred masked, socially distanced people, we spoke the Easter hymns (COVID precluded singing), said some prayers, and watched the sun's rays begin to transform the distant mountain into a shimmering glow. The proceedings were interrupted at the end of the service by the clearly identifiable, continuous call of a loon as it flew over the assembly. It was magnificent, partly because it was Easter morning, but mostly because in all my years of spotting and listening to loons, I have never seen one fly. I have read that it takes a quarter mile of open water and a distinct headwind for these large birds to get airborne. Loons don't often fly. But there it was, in incredible Easter glory. It was a rare delight.

The temptation that I felt, as I suspect many others did, was that the loon's appearance was a sign from God—for me, for us. That I could appropriate the flight of the loon to prove the Resurrection, because God sent the soaring loon at that moment. Which would then mean the experience was about me and not God; that this was happening at *my* campsite.

The loon's presence was a blessing, as were the service and the sunrise and the presence of so many people in the chilly early dawn. Ascribing the delight of the blessing to a purpose is an understandable temptation, but it short-circuits our ability to see in that we see everything through the lens of how it serves us. How it serves me.

I have long subscribed to the idea that the soul lives in the body. The good news of that is that there is something holy and incorporeal that lives inside us. The problem with it is the soul is then limited to self, giving rise to the idea that we have ownership of it. When a loon flies overhead on Easter morning it can confirm that misguided idea that it is meant for my or our soul, giving us a kind of dominion over the loon. As if the loon's flight is meant for me, for us.

Author and poet John O'Donohue has provided me with a different and transforming perspective. In his book *Anam Cara*, O'Donohue makes the ancient Celtic case that the body lives in the soul. For

O'Donohue, we inhabit a huge soul—which includes mountains and loons and bears. These manifestations are blessings—no more than that, and no less either. The blessings from that enormous soul keep coming— if we pay attention.

Which is what Mary Magdalene tries to do when she arrives at the tomb of Jesus on Easter morning (John 20:1–18). The stone has been rolled away. She runs to tell some of the disciples what she has seen, an unexpected development in this dramatic story that makes no sense to her. She thinks the body has been stolen. They all go back, the men arriving first. They rush into the tomb, see the linen wrappings rolled up, immediately believe in the Resurrection, and go home.

Mary doesn't leave. She can't, in part because she can't stop weeping, but mostly because she needs to spend more time figuring it out. Seeing some wrapped-up linens in the corner of the tomb is not enough for her. Two angels appear and ask why she is crying. Because, she plaintively says, "They have taken away my Lord, and I do not know where they have laid him." She turns around and sees Jesus, but she doesn't know that it is Jesus, because she can't imagine it is Jesus. She thinks the man she sees is the burial ground's gardener and challenges him to tell her where the body is. The man calls out to her by name, "Mary." She responds with "Rabbouni," a term of respect that is filled with love. Her attention span, longer than that of the disciples, enables her to join the men in having a life-changing experience, because she hung around long enough to recognize that the man she sees is indeed the risen Jesus. It often takes more than a moment to see differently.

Interpretations of the how and what of the Resurrection are as numerous as the number of Christian denominations and sects that have built their theologies and ministries upon it. There is uniform agreement, among believers and unbelievers, that Jesus was executed. His death is a matter of historical record. But his Resurrection poses a vast array of challenging questions: Did he emerge from the tomb with ten fingers and ten toes? Jesus does ask Thomas to put his hands in his wounds, but did that really happen (John 20:27)? At another Resurrection appearance, he tells his disciples, "Touch me and see; for a ghost does not have flesh and bones as you see that I have" (Luke 24:39). Were the flesh and bones real? Did he somehow become clairvoyant? Did he come to new life with some new invisible power that enabled him to enter locked upper rooms and miraculously rise up into heaven at the Ascension? Over the centuries these and other questions have yielded an endless litany of proposed answers that we continue to sift through, generating continuous debate.

There are some Christians who maintain that the man Mary saw was indeed the gardener. What was different was that Mary was now able to see the risen Christ in the gardener. Her eyes had been opened, because of the Resurrection, to see differently. To be able to see the presence of the risen Christ in everyone, including the gardener. To see that everyone is blessed because, as Catholic priest and author Richard Rohr has written, everyone has been blessed with the presence of the Cosmic Christ.

What is important here is less about the physics and biology of the Resurrection—how was he raised? and what was he raised as?—and more about the effect that the Resurrection has on us. Easter is an invitation to see differently: to have our eyes opened to recognize that we are all blessed by the gift of new life. Which means that people who are blessed can help open our eyes. That is what my friend Al did for me when he and I talked about the books we read while we hung out together at the outdoor soup kitchen in Newark. That is what so many of the other men at the soup kitchen, and their stories of courage and faith, did for me. That is what Santos Garcia did for me when I drove him to a shelter in New Jersey and he identified himself as a Christian. That is what the Japanese student did for me when he challenged my culturally limited view of the world. That is what the flying loon did for the Easter congregation in New Hampshire. The incidents, the experiences, go on and on. Inviting us to see blessing. Even in overwhelming darkness.

Guatemalan poet and theologian Julia Esquivel captures the unrelenting and horrific darkness that smothered her country in the wake of an American-instigated coup in 1954, a darkness that engulfed the country for decades. In her poem "They Have Threatened Us with Resurrection," written in 1980, she talks about the killings and disappearances of thousands of Guatemalan men and the rapes of countless women. The survivors can't sleep, not because of the drunks coming out of the bars, nor because of the fans at the ballpark or the tumult of the crowds who are heading up to the mountains:

What keeps us from sleeping is that they have threatened us with
    Resurrection!
Because every evening
Though weary of killings,
An endless inventory since 1954,
Yet we go on loving life
And do not accept their death! . . .

No brother,
It is not the noise in the streets
Which does not let us sleep.

Join us in this vigil
And you will know what it is to dream!
Then you will know how marvelous it is
To live threatened with Resurrection!

To dream awake,
To keep watch asleep,
To live while dying,
And to know ourselves already
Resurrected.

The survivors, who become witnesses for justice, can still see the presence of those who have been taken away:

Because they live
today, tomorrow, and always,
in the streets baptized with their blood,
in the jungle that hid their shadows,
in the river that gathered up their laughter,
in the ocean that holds their secrets,
in the craters of the volcanoes,
Pyramids of the New Day,
which swallowed up their ashes.

These survivors, most of whom are women, can see life, even in the face of constant death. They are threatened with Resurrection. Their ability to see new life has a power—and a hope. Their witness—to new life—has the capacity to open the eyes of others and at the same time to expose brutal injustice.

And provide us with the courage to do something about it.

That is an incredible blessing. May we live in its embrace—with our eyes opened.

ACKNOWLEDGMENTS

One of the privileges of the ordained life is the expectation that an audience, be it a congregation, a community, or a diocese, wants to hear or read about what I see—and what it all means to me and potentially what it means for them. For over forty years I have shared my images and thoughts in sermons, blog posts, articles, and essays—all of which are relatively short. There are a host of people who have encouraged me to stretch my writing—and my horizon—by putting my thoughts into a book.

I am grateful to Bob Morris, friend and spiritual guide for most of those forty-plus years, who encouraged me to keep writing about the ideas, images, and thoughts I felt compelled to write about. It all would cohere, he suggested, which is what has happened. My gratitude extends to David Rynick, a friend for thirty years, who dared me to share my initial writing with him, as he did with me—and we insisted to each other that we had stories to tell. To Bob Anderson, my college classmate and soul brother, who "workshopped" with me many times over several months, and who encouraged me to share more of my stories along with more stories from scripture. Thank you to Al Roxburgh, who consulted with the Diocese of Newark for several years when I served as bishop, and who taught me to pay more attention to seeing God in our communities and challenged me to focus my writing there. Miguel Escobar and I became writing partners for a time, and I so appreciate his tenderness and insight.

Nancy Bryan was not only my editor at Church Publishing, helping me to reframe some ideas and editing key portions of the text, but she offered gentle and consistent support for this first-time author.

Alan Bradshaw of Newgen Knowledge Works and his team provided challenging yet ultimately exquisite editorial advice.

Finally, I want to thank the many men who came twice a day to the outdoor feeding program at St. John's Church in Newark, New Jersey. Their courage, faith, and wisdom opened my eyes to look beyond what I expected to see.

BIBLIOGRAPHY

The Bible: New Revised Standard Version. New York: National Council of Churches, 1989.

The Book of Common Prayer. New York: Church Publishing, 1979.

* * *

Barker, Joel. *Discovering the Future: The Business of Paradigms.* Video. Gahanna, Ohio: ABC Training, 1988.

Berry, Thomas. *The Dream of the Earth.* New York: Random House, 1988.

Bingen, Hildegard. *Scivias.* Translated from 1152 text. New York: Paulist Press, 1990.

Bishop, Bill. *The Big Sort: Why the Clustering of Like-Minded America Is Tearing Us Apart.* Boston: Houghton Mifflin, 2008.

Branch, Taylor. *Parting the Waters: America in the King Years.* New York: Simon and Schuster, 1989.

Brueggemann, Walter. *The Prophetic Imagination.* Minneapolis: Fortress Press, 2001.

Brueggemann, Walter. *To Act Justly, Love Tenderly, Walk Humbly.* Mahwah, NJ: Paulist Press, 1986.

Coates, Ta-Nehisi. *Between the World and Me.* New York: Spiegel & Grau, 2015.

Esquivel, Julia. *Threatened with Resurrection: Prayers and Poems from an Exiled Guatemalan.* Translated by Ann Woehrle. Elgin, IL: Brethren Press, 1994 (second edition).

Giridharadas, Anand. *Winners Take All: The Elite Charade of Changing the World.* New York: Alfred A. Knopf, 2018.

King, Martin Luther, Jr. *Letter from Birmingham Jail.* New York: Bloomsbury Press, 1963.

Lamott, Anne. *Help, Thanks, Wow: The Three Essential Prayers.* New York: Penguin, 2012.

Lepore, Jill. "The Invention of the Police." *New Yorker,* July 20, 2020.

Lepore, Jill. *These Truths: A History of the United States.* New York: W. W. Norton, 2018.

Lincoln, Abraham. *Inaugural Address to Congress.* Washington, D.C.: Library of Congress, 1861.

Lupton, Robert. *Toxic Charity: How Churches and Charities Hurt Those They Help (and How to Reverse It).* New York: HarperCollins, 2012.

Madison, James. "Federalist Paper Number 10." *Daily Advertiser,* November 22, 1787.

Merton, Thomas. *Conjectures of a Guilty Bystander.* New York: Doubleday, 1968.

O'Donohue, John. *Anam Cara: A Book of Celtic Wisdom.* New York: Harper Perennial, 1998.

Palmer, Parker. *Let Your Life Speak.* San Francisco: Jossey-Bass, 2000.

Parker, Theodore. *Ten Sermons of Religion.* Boston: Crosby, Nichols and Co., 1853.

Plato. *The Republic.* New York: Simon and Schuster, 2010.

Sacks, Jonathan. *The Dignity of Difference.* London: Bloomsbury, 2003.

Sheldrake, Merlin. *Entangled Life: How Fungi Make Our Worlds, Change Our Minds and Shape Our Future.* New York: Random House, 2020.

Taylor, Barbara Brown. *Holy Envy: Finding God in the Faith of Others.* New York: HarperCollins, 2020.

Wallis, Jim. *The Great Awakening: Reviving Faith and Politics in a Post-Religious Right America.* New York: HarperOne, 2008.

Watson, Lilla. "Speech at United Nations Decade for Women's Conference." Nairobi, Kenya, 1985.

White, Micah. *The End of Protest: A New Playbook for Revolution.* Toronto: Penguin Random House, 2016.

Wilkerson, Isabel. *Caste: The Origins of Our Discontents.* New York: Random House, 2020.